AMAZING PAPER AIRPLANES

AMAZING PAPER AIRPLANES

THE CRAFT AND SCIENCE OF FLIGHT

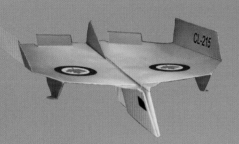

Kyong Hwa Lee

UNIVERSITY OF NEW MEXICO PRESS / ALBUQUERQUE

Library of Congress Cataloging-in-Publication Data
Lee, Kyong Hwa, 1937–
  Amazing paper airplanes : the craft and science of flight / Kyong Hwa Lee.
    pages cm
  Audience: Age 9–13.
  ISBN 978-0-8263-5664-2 (pbk. : alk. paper) — ISBN 978-0-8263-5665-9 (electronic)
  1. Paper airplanes—Juvenile literature. I. Title. II. Title: Paper airplanes.
  TL788.L44 2016
  745.592—dc23

                        2015025363

Cover photographs: *(top right)* Canadair CL-215, page 60; *(middle right)* Eurofighter Typhoon, page 68; *(bottom left)* Boeing 737 twin-engine jet airliner, page 73; *(top left)* Mirage 2000, page 62
Book Design: Catherine Leonardo
Composed in Minion Pro
Display is Gill Sans Std.

CONTENTS

Contents

Contents

PREFACE

PEOPLE HAVE ALWAYS admired things that have the ability to fly. At some time in their lives, many people have dreamed of soaring high in the sky like a bird or a plane. One way we can live part of that dream is to make other things soar and fly. A paper airplane is one of these things that almost anyone can make. Launching a paper airplane from our own hands and watching it soar through the air can give us a small glimpse of the satisfaction of flying.

Folding paper airplanes has been my lifelong hobby. It has always given me lots of joy, especially when I can create new modern-looking airplanes and watch them take flight. The act of folding paper is a fun activity in itself, and folding and flying paper airplanes with my grandchildren has been even more rewarding.

My website, amazingpaperairplanes.com, was created about fifteen years ago to share a collection of my designs with the Internet community. Since it was launched, the website has received worldwide recognition from Yahoo!, Science News Online, *Scientific American Frontiers* on PBS, WDR Fernsehen (German WebTV), and others.

From the visitor comments and e-mails I have received, I have learned that there is no age limit for paper airplane enthusiasts. People of all ages, from elementary school children to elderly grandparents, love to fold paper airplanes. Making paper airplanes can be an educational tool as well as just an enjoyable activity. I have received many comments from teachers who use paper airplanes as an educational tool in their science classes. I was also surprised to find that origami, a Japanese paper-folding art form, is used to promote brain development and rehabilitation in certain medical communities.

The paper airplanes presented in this book range from easy models to advanced designs. Many paper airplanes were designed to resemble actual airplanes. For these models I provide some information along with an image of the real airplane in the hope of expanding your interest in aerospace technology.

The introduction provides an orientation for beginner folders. Basic origami folding symbols and the theory of physics related to paper airplanes are presented. Those who do not want to wait to fold paper airplanes can skip the introduction and go right to chapter 1, the basic designs of paper airplane models. If you encounter any problems along the way, you can always come back to the introduction to get some help.

I hope this book provides you with a joyful, soaring experience in both the real world and your imagination!

(Note: To avoid injury, never fly any paper airplane in the direction of other people or animals!)

ACKNOWLEDGMENTS

I WOULD LIKE to thank the many people who have helped me prepare this book over the years.

First and foremost is my wife, Okchu, who continually motivated me to finish this book and who tirelessly cleaned up the fleets of scattered paper airplanes in our living room.

Second are my children, Jae and his wife, Julanie; Hae-Jung and her husband, Patrick; and David and his wife, Kristina, for their encouragement that I finish this book.

Third are my grandchildren—Jonathan, Janelle, Julian, Madeline, and Keegan—who inspired me by playing with my paper airplanes.

Thanks also to the many teachers, parents, and children worldwide who e-mailed me through my website (amazingpaperairplanes. com) to share their appreciation and stories of their experiences with my paper airplanes.

Finally, thanks to my son David for proofreading the manuscript and to the staff at the University of New Mexico Press for its editorial efforts in bringing this wonderful book together.

INTRODUCTION

WELCOME TO THE world of paper airplanes! This book will guide you through a number of creative paper airplane designs ranging from novice to advanced models. Many of the planes shown attempt to mimic real-world planes that you may have seen. In these cases, this book will provide some information on the real plane as well, to encourage your interest in aerospace technology.

This book has a number of sections in order to appeal to all types of readers. The most adventurous may choose to venture straight to the folding directions and start making paper airplanes. However, for those who are newer to paper airplanes, this book begins with an introduction to materials, basic folding symbols, and airplane terminology. For the scientifically minded, the science behind paper airplane flight is explained, but if you would like to go straight to folding planes, you can skip the theory sections or return to them later. Last but not least are the directions on how to fold paper airplanes.

Feel free to move around this book at your own pace, but always mind the one and only rule: Have fun!

Materials and Tools

Paper is, of course, the most important material for folding a paper airplane. Notebook or computer paper is very good for paper airplanes and is probably the easiest to find, but you can use other kinds of paper as well. Most of the paper airplane designs in this book are based on standard 8½ × 11-inch, US letter-size paper. If you have a different size of paper, don't worry—your planes may look slightly different (maybe narrower or wider), but it won't affect your flights too much.

Scissors may be useful for trimming your planes. If you photocopy the templates at the end of the book, you may also want to trim the borders of your copies so they have a neat edge. (Note: Younger children should always have adult supervision for this.)

Tape is an optional item but can be very useful for airplane designs that have many folds. It can help keep the correct shape of the paper airplane while you fold it.

The Two Basic Folds

The two basic folds are the *valley fold* and the *mountain fold*. They are nearly identical, but one (valley) will hide the fold line, and the other (mountain) will leave the fold line visible. That is, if you were to draw a line on a piece of paper, then valley fold on that line, you would no longer be able to see the line you drew after the fold was complete. If you did a mountain fold, the line would be visible on the crease once you were done.

A valley fold is done by bringing one side of the sheet up onto itself. The fold line is in a "valley" and not visible once the fold is complete because it is inside the folded paper. Note how you can create a valley fold from either the top or the bottom edge. Our paper airplane diagrams will use a dash line when you should use a valley fold. Note that the folding direction is shown with a triangle arrowhead.

The Valley Fold (Sequence A)

| 1 | 2 | 3 |

The Valley Fold (Sequence B)

| 1 | 2 | 3 |

The Mountain Fold (Sequence A)

| 1 | 2 | 3 |

The mountain fold is almost identical to the valley fold, except that you take one edge of the paper and fold it behind itself. Just like the valley fold, the mountain fold can be done with the paper either way: the top edge back under the bottom, or the bottom edge back under the top.

The important difference is that the fold line is visible on the outside of the paper once you are done with the fold. In our diagrams we will use a dash-dot line or a dash-dot-dot line to represent a mountain fold. Note that the folding direction is shown with a half-triangle arrowhead.

The Mountain Fold (Sequence B)

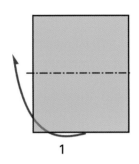

1

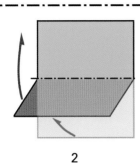

2

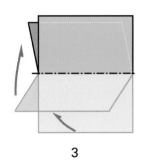

3

The Inside Reverse Fold

The next fold to learn is the *inside reverse fold*. This is a slightly more advanced fold that is often used to make the tail fin of paper airplanes. This fold gets its name from the fact that the original creases you make get reversed and placed inside the paper.

To perform this fold, begin with a sheet of paper folded in half. Steps 1 through 4 are used to crease the paper. In step 5, the paper is opened slightly, and the corner tip is pushed inside and in between the two outer layers of paper. Step 6 shows the completed inside reverse fold.

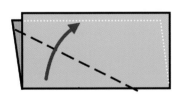
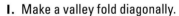

1. Make a valley fold diagonally.

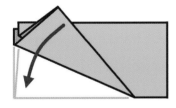

2. Crease, then unfold.

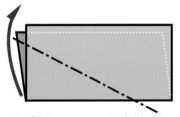

3. Make a mountain fold.

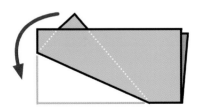

4. Crease, then unfold.

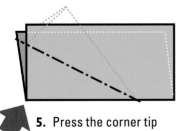

5. Press the corner tip into two layers.

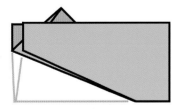

6. The inside reverse fold is complete.

Introduction

More Symbols and Signs

Shown below are the symbols and signs used in this book. You do not need to memorize these. They are listed here so that you may refer back to this page when you need to know the meaning of a symbol or a sign.

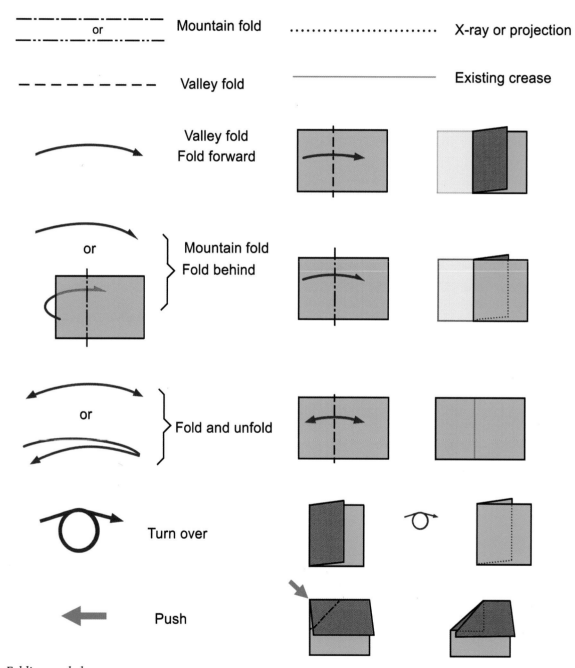

Mountain fold	X-ray or projection
Valley fold	Existing crease
Valley fold / Fold forward	
Mountain fold / Fold behind	
Fold and unfold	
Turn over	
Push	

Folding symbols

Paper Format Conversion

Depending on the paper you choose to use, you might need to cut it to the right size. Newspaper, advertising brochures, and other non-letter-size paper will have to be cut to the right width and height.

There are two width-to-height ratios that come in handy when folding paper airplanes.

Some planes require a 2 to 1 ratio, meaning that the paper is twice as long as it is wide. Other planes are better constructed with the International Standard A series, which has a ratio of 1.414 to 1. This means that for every inch of the width, the length will be 1.414 (the square root of 2) inches.

Let's start with directions on how to prepare a paper with a size ratio of 2 to 1:

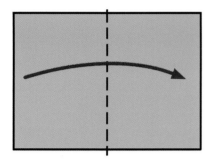

1. Fold the paper in half.

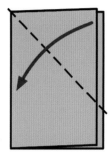

2. Bring the top corner to the side edge and flatten.

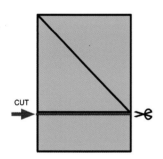

3. Cut the paper along the edge of the triangle flap and open the paper.

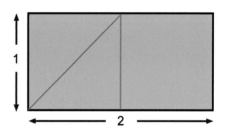

4. The paper has a size ratio of 2 to 1.

PAPER SIZE RATIO OF 2 TO 1

Here are the instructions for preparing paper using the International Standard A series, which has a size ratio of 1.414 to 1:

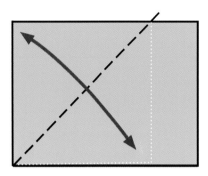

1. Fold the top left corner diagonally down to the bottom edge, crease, and unfold.

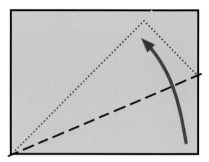

2. Fold the lower edge to the blue diagonal crease line.

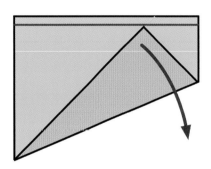

3. Mark a parallel line to the top edge through the corner of the top layer. Then unfold.

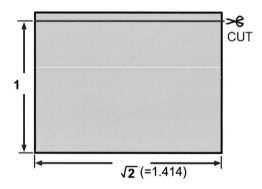

4. Cut the red marked line. Your 1.414 to 1 rectangle paper is ready.

PAPER SIZE RATIO OF 1.414 TO 1

Choosing the Best Paper

There are many different types of paper that you can use to fold your paper airplanes. However, there is no one best type of paper. The paper you choose can be any kind that creases well, is sufficiently strong enough to withstand repeated folding and unfolding, and is not too heavy. Computer paper, copier paper, and writing paper are some of the best choices. Recycled bond paper with a weight of about 20 pounds is excellent for paper airplanes.

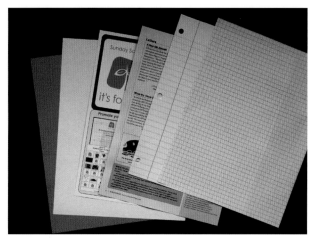

Paper selection. Left to right: colored paper, computer paper, advertisement sheet, magazine paper, filler paper, and quad paper

Heavier papers such as construction paper, watercolor paper, and pastel paper should be avoided unless you are folding for display and do not intend to fly your planes. Thinner or lighter papers such as newspaper tend to collapse as the size of the plane grows larger, but they may work for smaller-size planes. Try experimenting with different papers and sizes and see what works for you. Also keep in mind that sometimes the best paper is the kind you throw away as trash: computer printouts that are no longer needed, advertisements, or junk mail. Fold and fly away instead of throwing away!

The Best Folding Techniques

In addition to the paper, the way you make your folds can affect the flight of your paper airplanes. The best way to fold paper airplanes is on a hard, flat surface such as a tabletop or a desk. To make a well-constructed paper airplane, avoid folding paper on an uneven or rounded surface, on your lap, or on a soft surface like a carpet. Be sure to make accurate, crisp creases. Running your thumbnail across the crease can help.

Sharp creases are important to flying your planes because they help the plane cut through the air and minimize drag from air resistance. The front edge of the plane usually has a few layers of paper with a small amount of air trapped between them. If the folds on the wing edges are not crisp, the layers will not meet flat, and the amount of air between the layers will increase. This creates pockets of air that have a bubbling effect as the plane is in flight. This bubbling will increase turbulence and drag and prevent smooth flight.

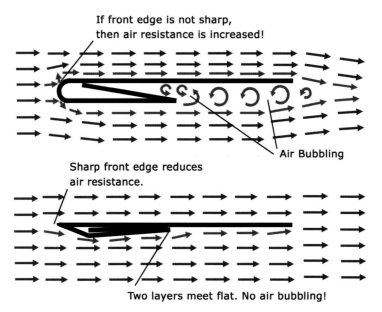

If front edge is not sharp, then air resistance is increased!

Air Bubbling

Sharp front edge reduces air resistance.

Two layers meet flat. No air bubbling!

The importance of sharp creases

Symmetrical accuracy of the wings is also very important for straight flight, so the two wings should be the same size and shape as each other as much as possible. If you fold poorly and one wing ends up slightly larger than the other, this will cause your airplane to veer to one side when it is thrown.

Accuracy in the first few steps of paper airplane folding is more important than at the later steps. Small errors in the first steps of folding often cause much larger problems at the later steps.

Flying Paper Airplanes

We usually expect paper airplanes to fly perfectly on the first throw. However, this almost never happens. The best way to make a plane really soar through the air is through a few test flights. From the first throw we can see how well it performs. Does it nose-dive or stall? Does it fly straight or turn to the left or the right?

Once you see what your plane is doing, you can make slight changes to improve the performance of the flight. You might be surprised by how much a little change can affect the plane's flight!

Four common problems and solutions are listed below. If you follow these guidelines, you should be able to adjust your paper airplane until it flies smoothly and straight.

- Plane nose-dives straight into the ground.
    You may have thrown too gently; try throwing a little faster.
    Bend the back of the plane (the trailing edges) upward. This will create an "elevator." (A later section will cover elevators in more detail.)
- Plane climbs too quickly, stalls, then falls to the ground.
    You may have thrown too hard; try a softer throw.
    Bend the back trailing edges of the plane down a little bit.
    Sometimes stalling happens when the nose of the plane is too light. Try

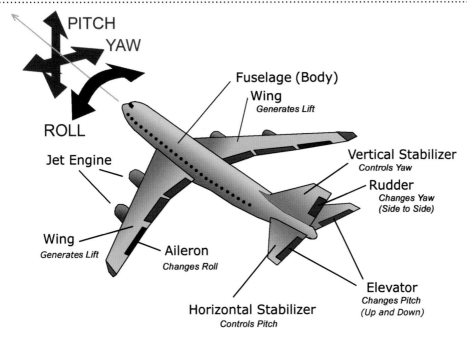

Airplane terminology

adding a paper clip to the nose (or between the nose and the center) of your plane.

- Plane veers off sharply to the left or right.

  Check both wings to make sure they are smooth, flat, and the same size and shape.

  If your plane has wing tips (like the Wildcat Fighter paper airplane), check to make sure that both wing tips are pointing straight up and are perpendicular to the wing.

- Plane rolls while flying.

  Check the profile of the wings to make sure they are the same size and shape.

  Hold the plane and look at it from the back. The wings should be flat or form a shallow V shape. Bend them upward a little bit if the plane has more of an M shape. This problem will be covered in more detail in the section on the dihedral angle.

Airplane Terminology

Let us review some aeronautical terms and the parts of an airplane before we discuss paper airplanes.

An airplane in flight may encounter disturbances and should remain stable against these unwanted forces. Most of the details you see on the wings and the tail fin will provide this stability. Three motions are used to describe the movement of a plane: yaw, pitch, and roll. *Yaw* is the left-to-right motion. *Pitch* is the upward or downward tilt of the nose of the plane. *Roll* occurs when the plane rotates around the fuselage (such as when the left or right wing tilts downward). Yaw, pitch, and roll are controlled by rudders, elevators (described in the next section), and ailerons (movable airfoils at the trailing edge of the wings), respectively.

The biggest difference between real airplanes and paper airplanes is that most paper airplanes do not have horizontal or vertical stabilizers.

9

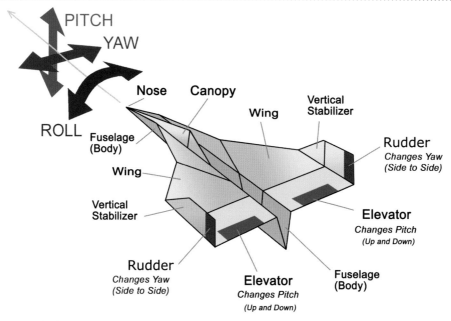

Paper airplane terminology

Instead, the larger wing surface provides lift and horizontal stability. Vertical stabilizers may be made from the tips of the wings. The fuselage also acts as a vertical stabilizer. There is no equivalent to an aileron to control roll in a paper airplane, but the effect can be mimicked by adjusting the elevators unevenly.

Elevators

Elevators are little flaps on the back edge of a plane that can be bent upward (a positive angle) or downward (a negative angle). Adjusting the elevators will affect how much lift the plane produces when it is thrown.

When a paper airplane is thrown into the air, there will be two opposing forces at work: the paper airplane will get lift from the wings while gravity will pull the plane down. The lift from the wings is what enables the plane to fly. To get this lift, the wings must be angled so that the air presses them upward as the plane flies through the air. The elevator is the most important part of the plane in achieving this lift.

Every plane should have at least a little adjustment of its elevators to get the best performance. The elevator angle is crucial. Too much angle will result in too much lift, increasing air drag and reducing speed until the plane can no longer stay in the air. Too little angle will cause your plane to nose-dive. The ideal amount of angle is usually ten to twenty degrees, but you will need to experiment to find out what will work best for your plane.

Not all planes will require small elevators cut into the wings. In fact, on many planes you can achieve the same effect by bending the back edge of the wings upward slightly.

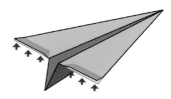

Creating an elevator by bending the wings

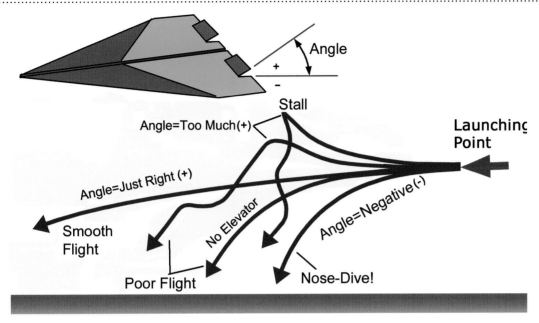

Elevator adjustments

The Dihedral Angle

When you look at your paper airplane from the nose or the tail, examine the angle between the wing and the horizontal line of the plane. This is called the *dihedral angle*. The dihedral angle is an important feature of a plane that will affect how it flies. When the wings are tipped upward from the horizontal line, this is called a *positive dihedral*. When the wings are below the horizontal line, this is called a *negative dihedral*, or *anhedral*.

Adjusting the dihedral is probably the most important thing to do before launching your plane. Paper airplanes with a positive dihedral angle will tend to stabilize in flight. A paper airplane that has a negative dihedral angle will tend to roll and become unstable.

Notice that when you are holding the plane, the dihedral angle will be different than when the plane is in flight. Be careful to look at the wing shape when you release the paper airplane from your hand to make sure that the wings stay in a flat position or a positive dihedral.

Vertical Stabilizers

Most real airplanes have a tail fin that acts as a vertical stabilizer. It helps the plane fly in a straight line rather than swinging to the left or

Positive Dihedral, Stable Condition

Negative Dihedral, (Anhedral), Unstable Condition

Dihedral and anhedral angles

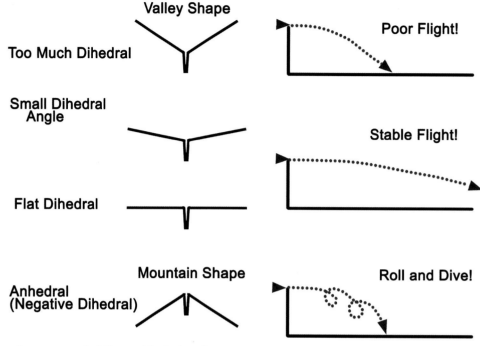

Flight performance with different dihedral angles

the right. The rudder attached to the rear edge of the tail fin can be moved from side to side and allows the plane to turn left and right.

Your paper airplane might not have a tail fin, but the body itself will usually act as a vertical stabilizer. If your plane needs additional stability, you can make vertical stabilizers by bending the wing tips up, as described earlier.

If a paper airplane is folded with perfect symmetry, it should fly straight and never turn to the left or the right. However, most paper airplanes are not perfectly symmetrical and will tend to veer to one side or the other when they are first thrown. This tendency can be fixed by adding a vertical stabilizer and bending the vertical edges to form a rudder. Air will push against the stabilizer and the rudder during flight. If you bend the rudder to the left, the tail of the plane will be pushed to the right and your plane will fly to the left. By the same token, if

you bend the rudder to the right, your plane will turn to the right.

Artwork

Paper airplanes can be fun to design, build, and launch. Artwork can enhance them: with colored pencils, crayons, or markers you can decorate a paper plane any number of ways. Try writing your plane's name on the side, for instance, or add a few military aircraft markings. Another idea is to use your favorite computer image software to make professional-looking paper planes.

If you need help getting started, you may use the predecorated paper artwork from my website, amazingpaperairplanes.com. There you will find templates that you can download and print out.

Full-color templates for all paper airplane models are provided in the appendix. You are welcome

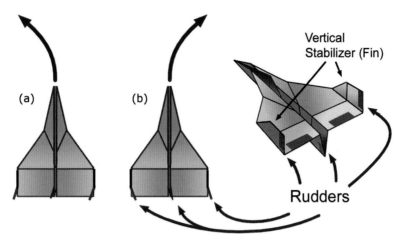

Yaw control with rudders

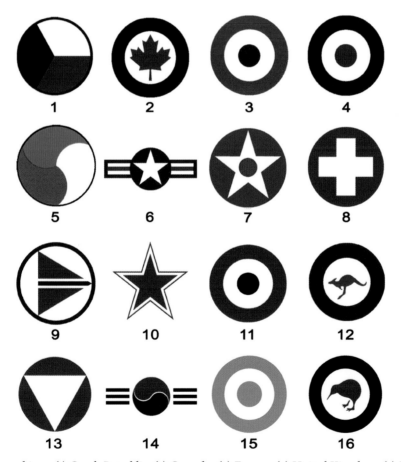

Military aircraft markings: (1) Czech Republic, (2) Canada, (3) France, (4) United Kingdom, (5) Ireland, (6) United States, (7) US Army Air Corps (1926–1941), (8) Switzerland, (9) Norway, (10) Russia, (11) Egypt, (12) Australia, (13) Austria, (14) South Korea, (15) Argentina, and (16) New Zealand

to make photocopies and use them when you fold the planes. The templates will make it much easier to fold your paper planes, and the finished models will be much more attractive.

The Theory of Flight

Paper airplanes have several forces at work as they cut through the air. *Thrust* is the force that makes the plane move forward, and it comes from your hand when you launch the plane into the air. The *weight* of the plane is a force created by gravity that pulls the plane toward the ground. *Drag* is the force from air resistance and pushes the plane in a direction opposite to the plane's motion. *Lift* is the force that pushes the plane up and keeps it in flight. The combination of these forces determines how well the plane flies through the air.

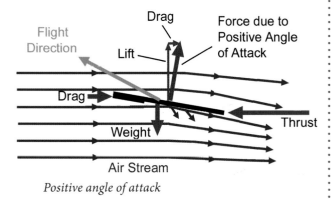

Positive angle of attack

Although thrust, weight, and drag are all key forces, the most essential force for flight is lift. A common misconception is that the shape of the wing is essential to generate lift. Real airplanes, however, generate lift by having a longer airstream over the top of the wings than under the bottom of the wings. This is known as Bernoulli's principle. However, a paper plane's wings are flat and cannot generate lift using this principle.

Instead, a paper plane generates lift by the

angle at which it flies through the air. The airstream hitting the underside of the wing is deflected toward the ground. Here Newton's third law of motion comes into play: "For every action there is an equal and opposite reaction." The opposite reaction in this case is a proportionally equal amount of force pushing the plane upward, generating lift.

When a plane is flying flat and level through the air, there is no angle between the airstream and the wings, no air deflection off the wings, and thus no lift. This plane will quickly fall to the ground.

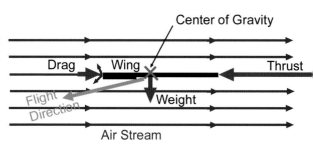

Zero angle of attack

We have determined that a positive angle is important to generate lift. However, increasing the angle also increases the amount of surface area that hits the air as the plane flies. This increases drag, which pushes against your plane as it flies through the air, reducing its speed. For a long-lasting flight, the angle has to be big enough to generate lift yet small enough not to make the plane slow down too much from drag. Adjusting the elevators is the key to this control.

The Center of Gravity and the Center of Lift

A well-designed paper airplane is one with good stability. Planes with good stability are able to return to their original flight orientation if they

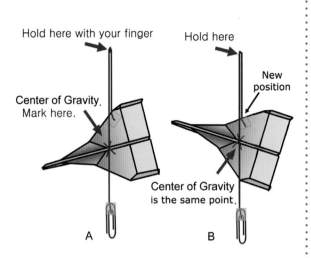

Finding the center of gravity

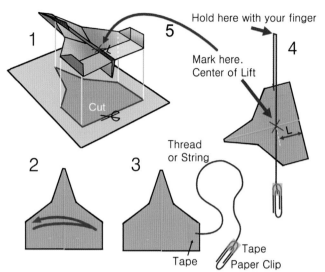

Finding the center of lift

are disturbed by some force. *Pitch stability* is perhaps the most important factor for smooth flight. A pitch-unstable airplane will either head up into a stall or nose-dive to the ground. A pitch-stable airplane, however, might oscillate up and down a few times when it is disturbed but will quickly settle back into smooth flight. The key to making a pitch-stable paper airplane is the proper setting of the center of gravity and the center of lift.

The *center of gravity* is the weight center where the plane will balance if you hold the plane loosely. You can locate the center of gravity more accurately with a paper clip, some thread or string, and a piece of tape. Attach one end of the thread or string anywhere on the edge of the plane with the tape, and attach the other end to a paper clip. Hold the middle of the thread with your finger and mark where the string crosses the center of the plane. No matter where you place the tape on the edge of the plane, you will get the same center of gravity.

The *center of lift* (also sometimes known as the *center of pressure*) is a little harder to find. It is the center of the wing area. To find the center of lift, you will need a piece of paper that is the exact shape of the wing. You can get this by tracing the plane's outline on a blank sheet of paper. Cut out the outline, then use the same technique you used to find the center of gravity with the tape, thread or string, and paper clip. That point on the plane is the center of lift. This technique may be easier if you use a slightly heavier paper, like a manila folder.

Now that you have both the center of gravity and the center of lift for your plane, you should make two measurements: the distance between the center of gravity and the end of the plane (L_1), and the distance between the center of gravity and the center of lift (L_3). (If the distance between the center of lift and the end of the plane is L_2, then $L_3 = L_1 - L_2$.) Once you have these numbers, you can calculate the relative position (RP) with the following formula:

$$RP = 100\% \ \times \ \frac{L_3}{L_1}$$

15

Introduction

The first rule for stable flight is that the center of gravity must be in front of the center of lift. The second rule is that the RP should be 30 to 40 percent. If the plane's RP is too small, the plane will probably be unstable and stall in flight. Your design will have to be modified to increase the weight in the front or reduce the weight in the back. If your plane's RP is too big, your plane will probably nose-dive. You might improve your design with elevators, but they can only help so much. The plane should probably be redesigned to have more weight in the back or less weight in the front.

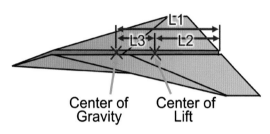

L1=12.6 cm   L2=8.0 cm   L3=4.6 cm

L3/L1(%)=100% x 4.6/12.6=36.5%

Calculating the relative position

CHAPTER ONE

BASIC DESIGNS

THIS CHAPTER PRESENTS the traditional, most basic paper airplane designs. They will allow you to gain confidence in folding before moving on to the more complex designs. If you face any unfamiliar symbol or sign, you should refer back to the "More Symbols and Signs" section in the introduction.

Classic Dart
Page 18

New Dart
Page 20

Classic Glider
Page 22

New Glider
Page 24

Flying Wing
Page 26

Square Wing
Page 28

Wildcat Fighter
Page 30

Delta Fighter
Page 33

Classic Dart

The Classic Dart is probably the oldest, most well-known paper airplane in the world. Its design is simple, easy to fold, and flies well. It is so named because it flies like a dart, fast and straight. The plane may have a slight tendency to nose-dive, but this can be corrected by bending the trailing edges of the wings upward. Optional elevators may be added for better flight control.

Folding Instructions

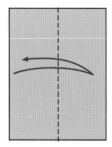

1. Use a sheet of letter-size paper. Fold the paper in half lengthwise and then unfold the paper.

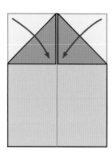

2. Lift the top corners and fold them down to the center crease, as indicated by the arrows.

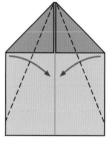

3. Lift each side corner and fold it to the center crease.

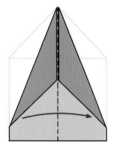

4. Make a valley fold in half. Turn the plane 90 degrees, as shown in the step 5 diagram.

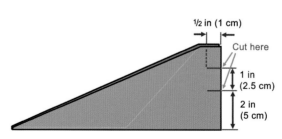

5. Cut the elevators as shown. The exact dimension is not required. (The cuts are optional.)

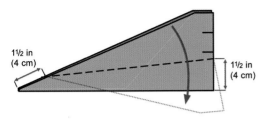

1½ in (4 cm)

1½ in (4 cm)

6. Create a wing crease that begins at the nose, as shown. Repeat for the other wing.

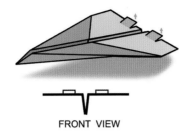

FRONT VIEW

7. Form a three-dimensional shape, as shown.

JIM ROSS

QF-106 Delta Dart (NASA, February 12, 1997)

The Convair QF-106, officially nicknamed the Delta Dart, has a large triangle wing just as the Classic Dart paper airplane does. QF-106s are operated as pilotless target drones, flown by remote control.

New Dart

The New Dart paper airplane is a variation of the Classic Dart model with a pilot's cockpit. The folding is still simple, yet it looks more like the real Delta Fighter. The pilot's cockpit acts like a vertical rudder, which increases the yaw stability and helps it fly straighter.

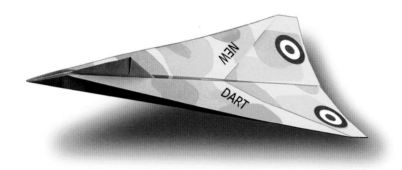

Folding Instructions

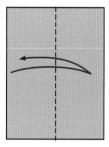

1. Use a sheet of letter-size paper. Fold the paper in half lengthwise and then unfold the paper.

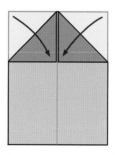

2. Lift the top corners and fold them down to the center crease, as indicated by the arrows.

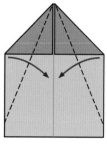

3. Lift each side corner and fold it to the center crease.

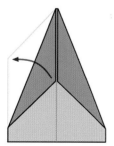

4. Unfold the left-side flap.

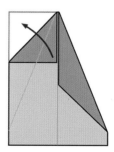

5. Unfold the top left-side triangular flap again.

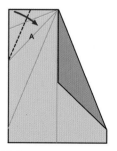

6. Fold the left corner to crease line A.

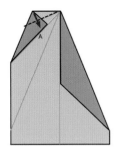

7. Fold the top left corner to crease line A.

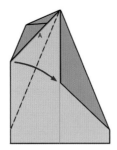

8. Fold the left-side flap again so that line A meets the center line.

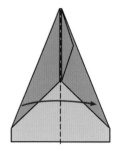

9. Fold the paper in half.

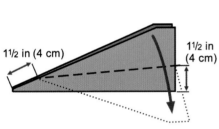

1½ in (4 cm)

1½ in (4 cm)

10. Fold the wing downward, as shown. Repeat on the other wing.

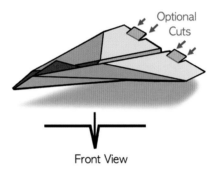

Optional Cuts

Front View

11. Adjust the wings to be flat, as shown. You may cut the elevators and bend them slightly up.

Classic Glider Type 1

The Classic Glider is perhaps the most well-known traditional paper airplane in Asian countries. It has a simple design, is easy to fold, and flies very well. This plane is nicknamed the Belly Button Plane because of the triangular lock at the fuselage. The standard model is a traditional design, but there is a variation with wider wings and vertical stabilizers.

Folding Instructions

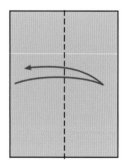

1. Use a sheet of A4 or 8½ × 11-inch, letter-size paper. Fold the paper in half lengthwise and then unfold the paper.

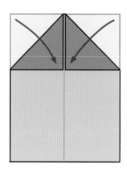

2. Lift each corner and fold it to the center crease, as indicated by the arrows.

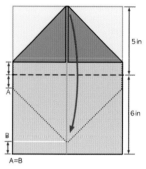

3. Bring the top corner downward to a point above the lower edge so that A = B (the dash line will be five inches from the tip if the paper size is 8½ × 11 inches).

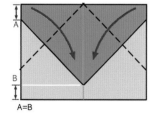

4. Lift each corner and fold it to the center crease, as indicated by the arrows.

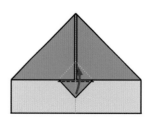

5. Fold the triangle tip upward to lock the two corners together.

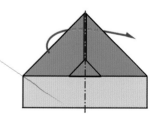

6. Use the center crease to mountain-fold the model in half. Turn the model around 90 degrees.

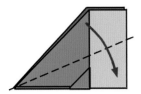

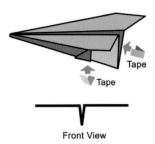

Tape

Tape

Front View

7. Fold the upper flap downward to the lower edge. Repeat on the other side.

8. Open both wings to 90 degrees.

9. The completed Classic Glider should look like this. You may tape the edges under the fuselage and the back of the plane. Adjust the wings until the plane has the profile shown in the front-view diagram.

Classic Glider Type 2

The Classic Glider variation has wider wings with vertical wing tips, and it glides better than the original model. After folding step 6, we follow steps 7A through 9A to complete this variation. Launch the plane with a gentle horizontal push. It will fly in a straight line and maintain a very long flight.

Folding Instructions

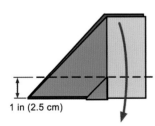

1 in (2.5 cm)

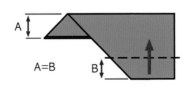

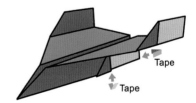

Tape

Tape

7A. Fold the upper flap down along the folding line parallel to the bottom edge. The folding line should meet the tip of the triangle lock. The valley fold line should be about 1 inch (2.5 centimeters) from the bottom edge.

8A. Fold up the wing tip. Note that the wing tip's height B is the same as the body's height A. Then open both wings.

9A. The Classic Glider type 2 paper airplane is complete. You may tape the edges under the fuselage and the back of the plane.

23

New Glider

The New Glider is a variation of the Classic Glider. It looks almost the same as the Classic Glider, but the triangular lock is unnecessary because of the elegant folds. The New Glider is a great plane for speed, distance, and accuracy.

Folding Instructions

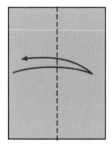

1. Use a sheet of A4 or 8½ × 11-inch, letter-size paper. Fold the paper in half lengthwise and then unfold the paper.

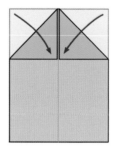

2. Lift each corner and fold it to the center crease, as indicated by the arrows.

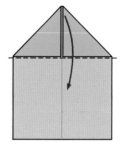

3. Bring the top triangular shape downward along the inside edge.

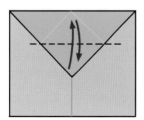

4. Fold the tip of the triangular shape to the top edge. Then crease and unfold.

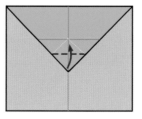

5. Fold the tip of the triangular shape to the creased line that was made in the previous step.

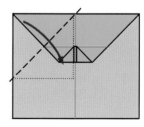

6. Fold the left corner to the center line.

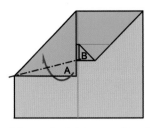

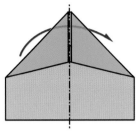

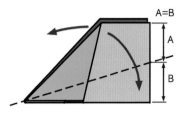

7. Mountain-fold upper flap A and tuck A under B.

8. Repeat steps 6 and 7 for the right side. Then mountain-fold the plane in half.

9. Make the wing folds.

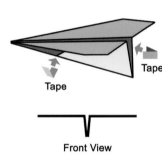

Tape

Tape

Front View

10. The completed plane should look like this. You may tape the edges under the fuselage and the back of the plane. Adjust the wings until the plane has the profile shown in the front-view diagram.

Flying Wing

The Flying Wing is one of the most unusual paper airplane designs. It was inspired by the experimental flying wing of the National Aeronautics and Space Administration (NASA). It is very simple to fold, but it may be a little difficult to throw at first. Once you master how to launch this plane, it is a lot of fun.

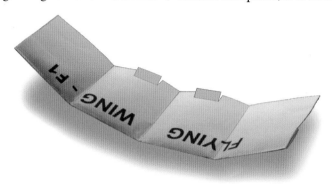

Folding Instructions

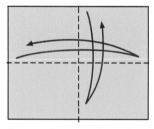

1. Crease the paper in half vertically and horizontally.

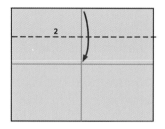

2. Fold along line 2 so that the top edge meets the center line.

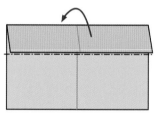

3. Mountain-fold along the center line and turn the paper over.

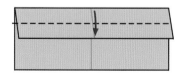

4. Fold the top section in half.

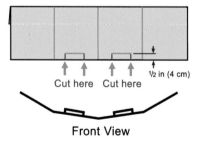

Front View

5. Turn the paper over and crease the model in half and unfold. Fold the left and right edges to the center line and crease them, as shown. Adjust the wing to match the profile. Make elevators, as shown with red lines, and bend up.

6. You are ready to launch the Flying Wing.

Solar-electric Helios Flying Wing (NASA, June 7, 2003)

Helios, a real Flying Wing, is a solar-powered, remotely piloted airplane, also known as an unmanned aerial vehicle, or UAV. It was built by NASA to develop the technologies that would allow long-term, high-altitude aircraft to serve as atmospheric satellites.

Square Wing

The Square Wing is good for long-lasting flights. A paper plane based on this design once held the world record for time aloft in flight. The vertical tail fin is optional. If you do not want to use scissors, you may skip the cutting step. However, the additional tail fin will give extra stability. The Square Wing is also known as a good plane for stunts.

Folding Instructions

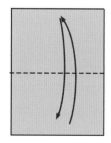

1. With the patterned side facedown, fold the paper in half. Crease the center line and unfold.

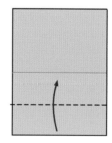

2. Fold the bottom edge to the center line.

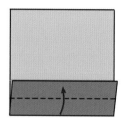

3. Fold the bottom edge to the center line again.

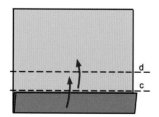

4. Fold the bottom edge along center line c shown in the diagram. Repeat folding along line d.

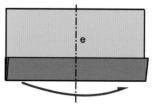

5. Mountain-fold the model along the vertical center line e.

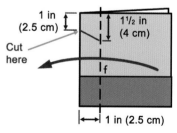

6. Cut the red line for the tail fin section. (This cut is optional.) Valley-fold the model along vertical line f.

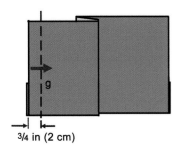

3/4 in (2 cm)

7. Valley-fold the model along vertical line g.

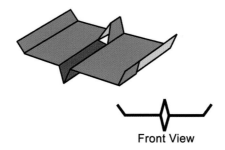

Front View

8. Repeat steps 6 and 7 on the right side. Adjust the wings and push the tail fin up to match the profile.

Wildcat Fighter Type I

The Wildcat Fighter looks like the Square Wing, but its fuselage is quite different. Its design was inspired by the famous Grumman F4F Wildcat fighter, the US Navy's most widely used carrier-based fighter during the first year and a half of World War II. This plane has a square wing and a short fuselage. The paper plane is easy to fold and is good for stunts and long-lasting flight. You can make this model more closely resemble the real Wildcat airplane by a few simple extra cuts.

Folding Instructions

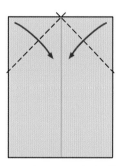

1. Crease the paper in half vertically. Fold the top corners to the center crease.

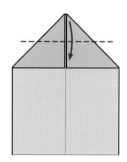

2. Fold the top point down to the inside corners.

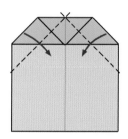

3. Fold the top corners to lie on the tip of the triangle section.

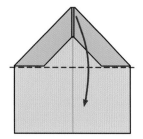

4. Fold the top triangular shape downward along the inside edge.

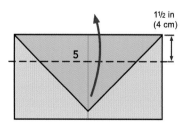

5. Fold the triangle part up along line 5.

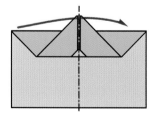

6. Mountain-fold the paper in half.

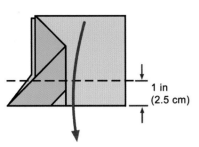

1 in
(2.5 cm)

7. Fold the wings down.

Profile

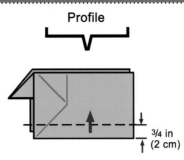

³/4 in
(2 cm)

8. Fold the wing tips up. Adjust
the wings to match the profile.

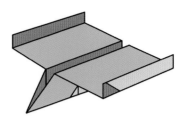

9. You now have a completed
Wildcat.

Wildcat Fighter Type 2

An additional cut at step 7 can make the Wildcat
Fighter an even more realistic World War II
plane. Then follow steps 10 and 11.

Folding Instructions

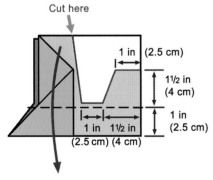

Cut here

1 in (2.5 cm)

1½ in
(4 cm)

1 in
(2.5 cm)

1 in   1½ in
(2.5 cm) (4 cm)

10. Cut along the red line, as shown,
and fold the wings down.

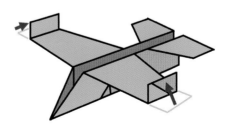

11. Fold the wing tips up, as in step 8.
The model is complete.

General Motors F4F Wildcat Fighter

The Grumman F4F Wildcat was the only effective fighter available to the US Navy and Marine Corps in the Pacific during the early part of World War II. The Wildcat had outperformed in the battle against the much faster, more maneuverable Japanese Zero fighter.

Delta Fighter

The Delta Fighter may look very much like the New Dart model, but its design is quite different. The center of gravity has been moved forward to improve the plane's stability. The Delta Fighter glides very well if you launch it a little bit faster. As usual, you can bend up the trailing edge of the wing for better flight.

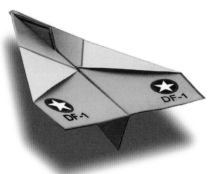

Folding Instructions

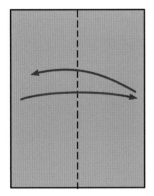

I. With the patterned side face-down, crease the center line vertically and unfold.

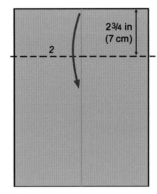

2. Fold the top edge down along line 2 (2¾ inches, or 7 centimeters, down from the top edge).

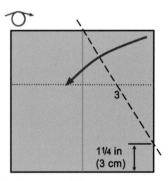

3. Fold the top right corner along line 3.

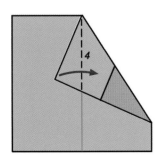

4. Fold the top layer along line 4.

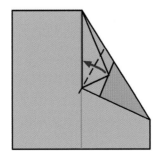

5. Fold the top layer corner to the center.

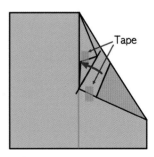

6. Tape the folds as shown.

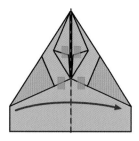

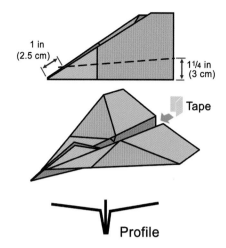

1 in (2.5 cm)

1¼ in (3 cm)

Tape

Profile

7. Repeat steps 3 through 6 for the left side. Then fold the model in half.

8. Use a ruler for the wing folding and fold the wings down. Adjust the creases until the model has the profile shown. Tape the tail section and bend the trailing edge up slightly for the best flight.

DAVID CHERKASOV

Dassault Mirage 2000–9EAD, United Arab Emirates Air Force (airliners.net)

The Mirage jet fighter is a famous French-made delta wing jet (delta is a Greek letter that looks like a triangle). A delta wing is considered to be a good choice for high-speed flight. The Mirage 2000 has a large high-lift wing that shortens the plane's takeoff distance.

CHAPTER TWO

SIMPLE DESIGNS

THE PAPER AIRPLANES in this chapter are very simple models, like the traditional paper airplanes in the previous chapter. However, these look more like real airplanes. All of them fly very well. You will need to use tape and scissors to make better-looking paper airplanes.

Space Shuttle—Type 1
Page 36

Twin Mustang
Page 40

F-117 Nighthawk
Page 44

Twin Tailfin
Page 49

Space Shuttle—Type 2
Page 38

B-2 Spirit
Page 42

SR-71 Blackbird
Page 47

F-102 Delta Dagger
Page 51

Space Shuttle—Type 1

The Space Shuttle resembles the NASA space shuttle orbiter. This origami plane is simple to fold and glides very well. It is a slow glider, so toss it gently for better flight.

Folding Instructions

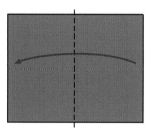

1. With the colored side up, fold the paper in half crosswise.

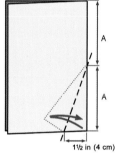

2. Fold the right-side corner and unfold. This will be the tail fin.

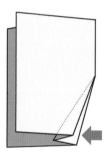

3. Insert the bottom corner inward as shown.

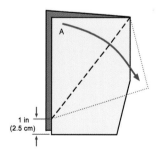

4. Fold side A diagonally down along the line shown in the pattern.

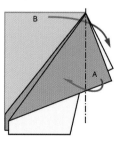

5. Repeat step 4 for side B. Make a mountain fold for side A along the vertical line. Repeat the same fold for side B.

6. Your paper should look like this. Turn the paper over and rotate 90 degrees.

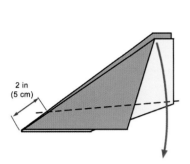

2 in
(5 cm)

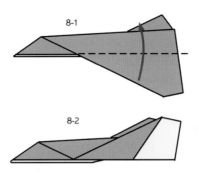

8-1

8-2

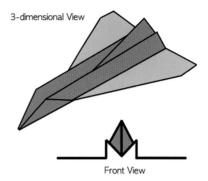

3-dimensional View

Front View

7. Fold the top flap downward. Repeat at the rear.

8. Lift the wings up.

9. Adjust the creases to match the front-view profile. Bend the trailing edge slightly up. The plane is ready to launch.

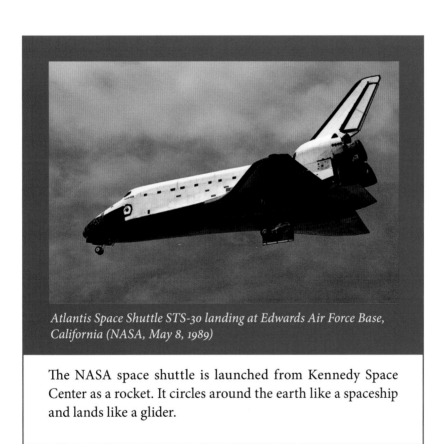

Atlantis Space Shuttle STS-30 landing at Edwards Air Force Base, California (NASA, May 8, 1989)

The NASA space shuttle is launched from Kennedy Space Center as a rocket. It circles around the earth like a spaceship and lands like a glider.

Space Shuttle—Type 2

The Space Shuttle type 2 model resembles the NASA space shuttle orbiter. This plane is simple to fold and glides very well. The tail fin requires cutting to make the plane more stable compared to the Space Shuttle type 1 model. It is a slow glider, so toss it gently during launch for better flight.

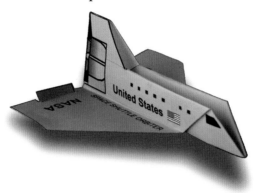

Folding Instructions

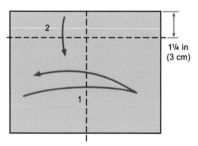

1. Start with the paper in landscape format. With the colored side down, crease center line 1. Fold the top side down along line 2.

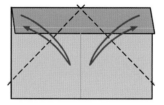

2. Fold the top corners inward to the center crease and unfold.

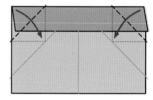

3. Fold the top corners to the sloping crease line.

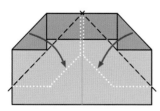

4. Fold the top left and right sides inward again using the crease line made in step 2.

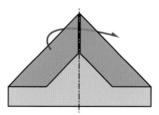

5. Mountain-fold the paper in half.

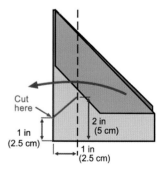

6. Cut the paper, as shown, along the red line for the tail fin. Fold the top wing to the left. Repeat the folding for the other wing.

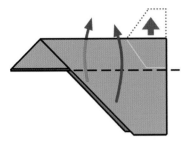

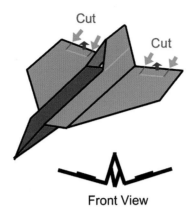

Cut

Cut

Front View

7. Fold the wings up along the edge of the fuselage. Bring the tail fin up.

8. Make elevators, as shown, and bend up. Adjust the model to match the front-view profile. Now the plane is ready to launch.

SCA transporting shuttle Discovery (NASA, May 8, 1989)

The Shuttle Carrier Aircraft (SCA) is an extensively modified Boeing 747 airliner that NASA has used to transport the space shuttle orbiters. The SCA was used to ferry the space shuttles from their landing sites back to the Shuttle Landing Facility at the Kennedy Space Center, as well as to and from other locations too distant for the orbiters to be delivered by ground transport.

Twin Mustang

The Twin Mustang resembles two paper airplanes joined together like the North American F-82 Twin Mustang. This paper airplane flies very well. However, you will find that its flight behavior changes a lot depending on the shape of the wing profile, so be sure to try several different profiles and experiment to see what works best for you.

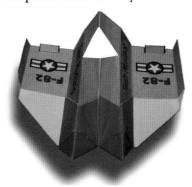

Folding Instructions

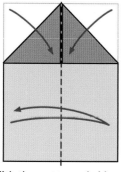

1. With the patterned side facedown, fold the paper in half, crease, and unfold. Then bring the top corners to the center creased line.

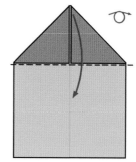

2. Fold the tip down along the edge of the top layers. Turn the model over for the next step.

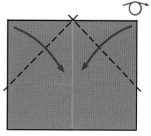

3. Fold the top corners down to the center line. Turn the model over.

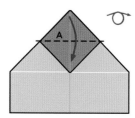

4. Fold the top corner along line A to the center crease and turn over the model.

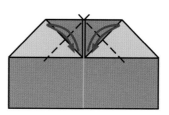

5. Fold the top layer corners out to the side, crease, and unfold.

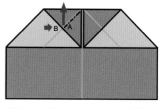

6. Bring side A upward while pressing side B. Note diagram 7 for this folding. Repeat for the right side.

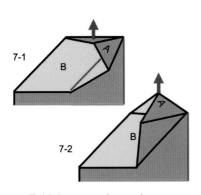

7-1

7-2

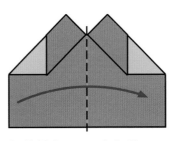

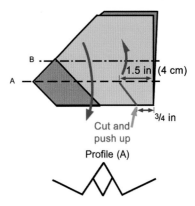

B

A

1.5 in (4 cm)

³/4 in

Cut and push up

Profile (A)

7. Fold the nose tip as shown.

8. Fold the paper in half.

9. Cut the red-line section and push up the tail fin. Fold both wings down along line A and mountain-fold along line B. Adjust the creases until the model has this profile, or try the second profile for your experiment.

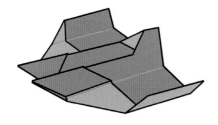

Profile (B)

The North American XF-82 in flight (US Air Force)

The F-82 appears to have two P-51 Mustang fuse-lages on one wing, but in reality it was a totally new design. Its purpose was to provide a fighter carrying a pilot and a copilot or navigator. In 1950, Japan-based F-82s were among the first US Air Force aircraft to operate over Korea.

B-2 Spirit

This B-2 Spirit is a good indoor glider. It glides very slowly and gracefully. With minor cuts we can make a double-W trailing edge just like the one on the Northrop Grumman B-2 Spirit, an American strategic bomber. But cutting is optional—the origami model is still the best glider.

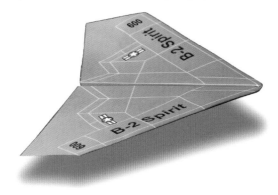

Folding Instructions

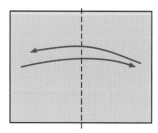

I. With the patterned side face-down, fold the paper in half, crease, and unfold.

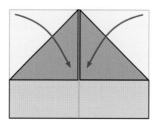

2. Bring the top corners to the center crease line.

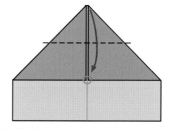

3. Fold the top point down to the circle, as shown.

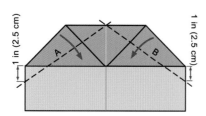

4. Use a ruler to draw folding lines A and B as shown. Fold both sloping parts along lines A and B.

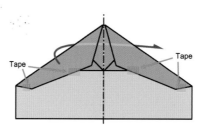

5. Tape as shown, then mountain-fold in half.

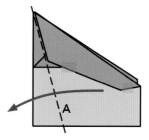

6. Fold the wing down along line A, as shown. Repeat on the other side.

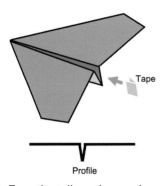

Profile

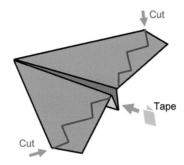

7. Tape the tail section as shown. Adjust the wings to match the front-view profile.

8. If you like the shape of the real B-2 Spirit, sketch double-W cutting lines with a pencil, then cut along the lines. The exact shape of the double W is not important, but you should make them symmetrical on both sides.

The B-2's first public flight at Edwards Air Force Base, California, July 17, 1989 (US Air Force)

The B-2 is a flying-wing airplane, which means it has no fin or fuselage. It features a serrated trailing edge and a blended (tadpole-like) fuselage. It is the most expensive type of aircraft yet built ($929 million in 1997). There are twenty B-2s in service with the US Air Force, which plans to operate the B-2 until 2058.

F-117 Nighthawk

The Nighthawk is so named because it resembles the Lockheed F-117 Nighthawk, a stealth ground-attack airplane formerly operated by the US Air Force. The pyramid-shaped cockpit canopy and swept wings are key features of this paper plane. With simple cutting, we can make a double-V shape trailing edge, which makes the paper plane more similar to the real F-117 stealth fighter. The plane glides very gracefully, with the hidden vertical stabilizer helping flight stability.

Folding Instructions

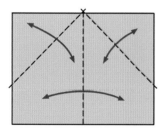

1. With the patterned side facedown, fold the paper in half and unfold. Fold in the top corners and unfold.

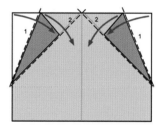

2. Fold both corners along line 1 and fold over along the line 2 creases.

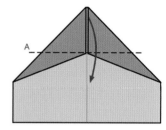

3. Fold down the tip along line A.

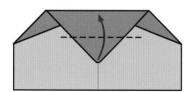

4. Fold the tip up to the top edge.

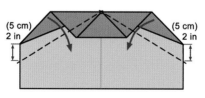

5. Fold the sloping edges along the folding lines, as shown.

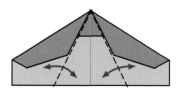

6. Make two creases by folding and unfolding along the sloping edge of the top layer.

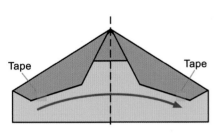

7. Fold the paper in half. You may use tape to hold the wings, as shown.

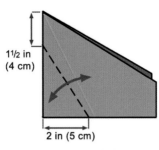

1½ in (4 cm)

2 in (5 cm)

8. Fold the bottom left corner and unfold.

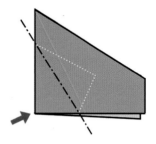

9. Push the bottom corner into two layers (inside reverse fold).

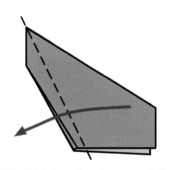

10. Fold the wing downward. Use the crease line made in step 6. Repeat on the other wing.

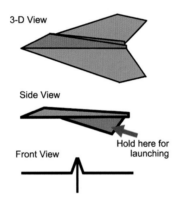

3-D View

Side View

Front View

Hold here for launching

11. Adjust the creases so that the model has the profile shown.

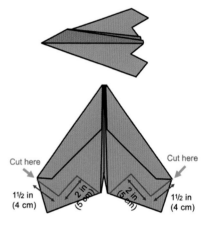

Cut here

Cut here

1½ in (4 cm)

2 in (5 cm)

2 in (5 cm)

1½ in (4 cm)

12. If you want the wing shape of the F-117, cut the trailing edge as shown. The exact dimension is not necessary.

CHAD THOMAS—JETWASH IMAGES

Lockheed F-117A Nighthawks in flight over New Mexico, May 13, 2004 (airliners.net)

The Lockheed F-117A Nighthawk's official name is actually Night Hawk, but the alternative one-word form is frequently used. Before the plane was given an official name, the engineers and test pilots referred to it as the Cockroach because it was hidden during the daylight to avoid detection by Soviet satellites. This name is still sometimes used. The Nighthawk's unique features include swept butterfly fins and low-swept wings blended into an angular fuselage.

SR-71 Blackbird

The Blackbird is a fast paper airplane because of its narrow wings. It has vertical stabilizers on the middle of the wings that make it resemble the Lockheed SR-71 Supersonic Blackbird. If your plane starts to nose-dive, you should bend up the plane's trailing edge for smooth flight. Do not throw this plane toward other people or animals—its nose is very sharp!

Folding Instructions

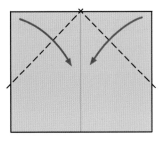

1. With the patterned side face-down, crease the center line crosswise and unfold. Bring the top corners to the center crease line.

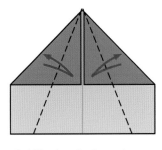

2. Fold in the sloping edges to the center crease line and then unfold.

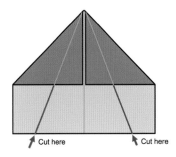

3. Cut the red-line creases.

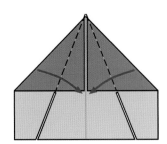

4. Fold in the sloping edges to the center crease.

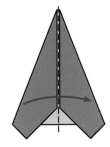

5. Fold in half.

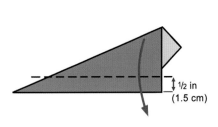

6. Fold down the wings.

47

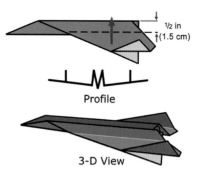

1/2 in
(1.5 cm)

Profile

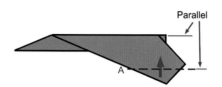

Parallel

A

3-D View

7. Fold up the top layer of the wing tip. Folding line A has to be parallel to the fuselage.

8. Fold up the wings and adjust the model to match the profile shown. Bend up the trailing tip slightly if the plane nose-dives.

JUDSON BROHMER

SR-71 Blackbird (NASA, December 1994)

The Lockheed SR-71 Blackbird is a long-range, advanced, strategic reconnaissance airplane. Its first flight took place on December 22, 1964. Throughout its nearly twenty-four-year career, the SR-71 was the world's fastest and highest-flying operational airplane.

Twin Tailfin

The Twin Tailfin paper airplane design is inspired by the North American B-25 Mitchell bomber, a twin-engine medium bomber with twin tail fins.

The Twin Tailfin paper plane is easy to fold, but it requires some cutting for the tail fins. Without cutting, the plane looks very much like the Wildcat Fighter type 1 (see chapter 1). It flies well even without tail fins.

Folding Instructions

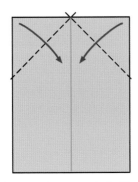

1. Crease the paper in half vertically. Fold the top corners to the center crease.

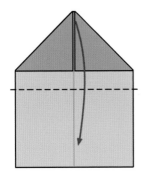

2. Fold the top point down to the bottom edge.

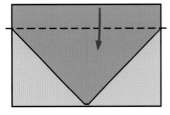

3. Fold the top edge down along the line at the triangle corner.

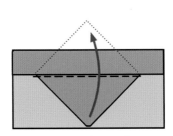

4. Fold the triangle section up.

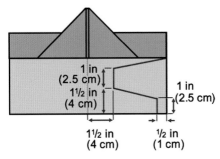

5. With a pencil and a ruler, draw the cutting line as shown.

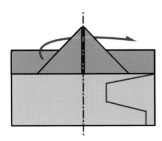

6. Mountain-fold the paper in half.

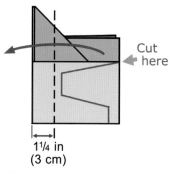

Cut
← here

1¼ in
(3 cm)

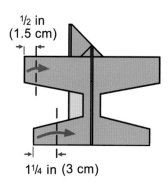

½ in
(1.5 cm)

1¼ in (3 cm)

3-D View

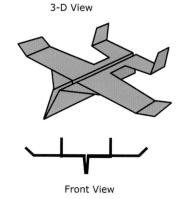

Front View

7. Cut both papers along the cutting line. Then fold the wing along the fuselage line.

8. Fold up the tail fin and bend the wing tip. Repeat for the other wing.

9. Adjust the creases to match the front-view profile. Bend the trailing edge a little upward for better flight.

MARK SHERWOOD

A US Army Air Force North American B-25C Mitchell bomber in flight near Inglewood, California (Library of Congress)

The North American B-25 Mitchell was manufactured by North American Aviation. It was used by the Allied air forces during World War II and by many other air forces after the war ended for four decades. It has a twin tail that gives the dorsal gunner an enhanced firing area. The twin tail also gives a better degree of redundancy: if one tail is damaged, the other may remain functional. The B-25 was named in honor of General Billy Mitchell, a pioneer of US military aviation. By the end of the B-25's production, nearly ten thousand had been built in numerous models.

F-102 Delta Dagger

The Delta Dagger is a sharp-looking paper airplane made to resemble the Convair F-102 Delta Dagger, which was the first supersonic delta wing interceptor airplane of the US Air Force. This design has two versions. One is a pure origami paper airplane that has no tail fin, whereas the second one requires a few cuts but more closely resembles the real F-102 Delta Dagger and has better roll stability because of the added triangle-shaped fin.

Folding Instructions

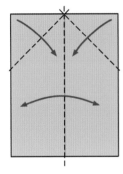

1. With the patterned side face-down, fold the paper in half and unfold. Fold the top corners to the center crease.

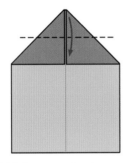

2. Fold the top point down to the inside corners.

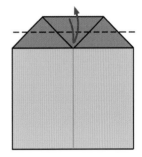

3. Bring the top edge to the edge of the top layers. Crease and unfold the paper.

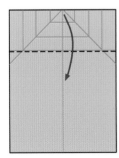

4. Fold the top part down along the third crease (horizontal dotted line).

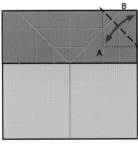

5. Fold the top right corner as shown. Top edge B should meet crease line A. Make a firm crease by repeating the valley and mountain folds.

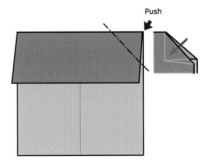

6. Push the right corner to make an inside reverse fold.

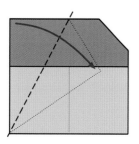

7. Fold the left side of the paper along the line between the bottom left corner and the top center crease line.

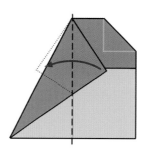

8. Fold the top layer flap along the center crease line.

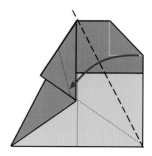

9. Fold the left side of the paper along the line between the bottom left corner and the top center crease line.

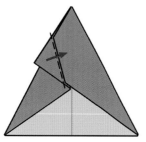

10. Insert the left side flap into the top layer pocket that was made by the inside reverse fold in step 6.

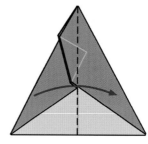

11. Fold the model in half.

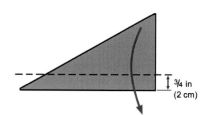

¾ in (2 cm)

12. Draw a line (¾ inch above the edge) for the fuselage as shown in the diagram. Fold down the top layer along this line.

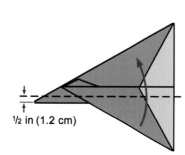

½ in (1.2 cm)

13. Draw a line ½ inch below the fuselage's top edge and fold up the wing. Repeat steps 12 and 13 for the other wing.

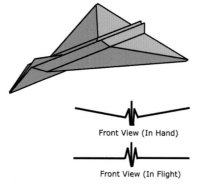

Front View (In Hand)

Front View (In Flight)

14. Open the wings and adjust the profile as shown. Bend up the trailing edge of the wings for better flight. The plane is ready to fly.

Optional Steps

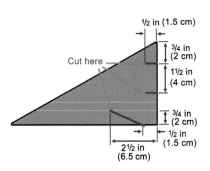

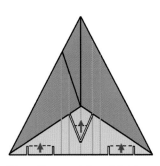

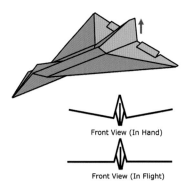

Front View (In Hand)

Front View (In Flight)

15. For a better-looking model, return to step 12 and cut the red lines as shown.

16. Open the model and fold up the tail part of the fuselage. Bend up the elevator tabs about 45 degrees.

17. Fold the model in half and repeat steps 12 and 13. Push up the tail fin and adjust the profile as shown. After some test flights, adjust the elevator angle for the best flight.

Convair F-102 Delta Dagger (US Air Force)

The main purpose of Convair's F-102 Delta Dagger, which entered service in 1956, was to intercept invading Soviet bomber fleets during the Cold War. One thousand F-102s were built.

CHAPTER THREE

INTERMEDIATE DESIGNS

THE DESIGNS IN this chapter are for very modern-looking origami paper airplanes. The folding is slightly harder than it was for the airplanes in the previous chapter. However, these look even more like real airplanes. All of them fly very well.

Concorde Airliner
Page 56

Seaplane
Page 58

Mirage Fighter
Page 61

F-5 Freedom Fighter
Page 63

Eurofighter Typhoon
Page 66

F-4 Phantom Jet
Page 69

Twin-Engine Airliner
Page 71

Twin Prop
Page 74

Concorde Airliner

The Concorde Airliner paper airplane design is inspired by the Concorde supersonic jetliner. Its distinctive features, which include a sharp nose and delta wings, closely resemble the real Concorde. You can even bend the nose down to imitate the droopy nose seen when the real Concorde approaches the runway. This model requires a little bit more accuracy than the previous models when you fold it. The use of a ruler for accurate measurement and a pencil to draw folding lines will help you get better results. Some clear cellophane tape may be useful as well.

Folding Instructions

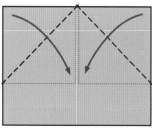

1. With the colored side face-down, fold the paper in half crosswise, crease, and unfold. Then bring the top corners to the center creased line.

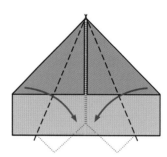

2. Fold in the sloping edges to the center line.

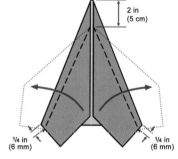

3. Using a ruler and a pencil, mark two points for the folding line ends, then draw the folding lines. Fold out the wings. Valley-fold the paper in half. Then turn the model 90 degrees counterclockwise.

4. Valley-fold the paper in half. Then turn the model 90 degrees counterclockwise.

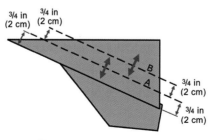

5. Using a ruler and a pencil again, draw two parallel lines, A and B, as shown. Fold each line twice, first in a valley fold, then mountain fold. Unfold. You have made two crease lines for a later step.

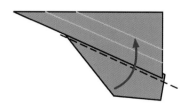

6. Fold up the wings.

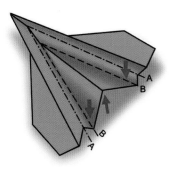

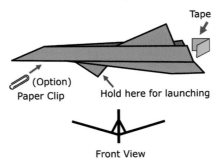

Tape

(Option)
Paper Clip

Hold here for launching

Front View

7. This step makes a tail fin. Open the model. Push down line B so that it makes a valley fold and line A becomes a mountain fold.

8. A piece of tape may be used to hold back part of the body. Adjust the wings to get a positive angle (dihedral), as shown. This will help the roll stability. Hold the triangle flaps at the bottom for launching. If the plane has a tendency to stall, insert a paper clip at the front of the fuselage.

RICHARD VANDERVORD

British Aircraft Corporation Concorde 102 Aircraft at Heathrow Airport, London (airliners.net)

The Concorde, designed by Britain and France, was the only supersonic passenger jet airliner that flew between Europe and the United States. It was the fastest commercial passenger airplane. Its maximum speed was Mach 2.4, which means it traveled 2.4 times faster than the speed of sound. Its flight time from Paris to New York is only three hours and forty-five minutes, whereas other aircraft, like the Boeing 747, take almost eight hours. All Concordes are now retired after twenty-five years of passenger service and nearly thirty-five years of flight. They have gone to their final resting places at museums around the world.

Seaplane

A seaplane is a type of aircraft designed to take off from water and land on water. There are two kinds of seaplanes: the floatplane and the flying boat. A floatplane has slender pontoons (flat-bottom boats) mounted under the fuselage. In the flying boat, the fuselage acts much like a boat. Most flying boats have small floats on the wings to keep them stable. This paper plane resembles the flying boat that has small floats on the wings.

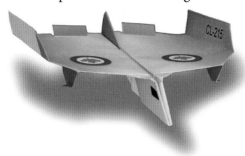

Folding Instructions

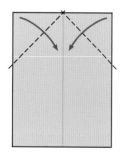

1. Start with 8½ × 11-inch paper. Fold the paper in half crosswise and unfold. Then fold the top corners inward to the center crease.

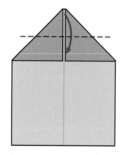

2. Fold the top point down to the inside corners.

3. Fold the top corners so they lie on the tip of the triangle section.

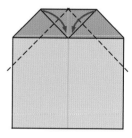

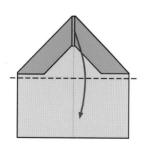

4. Fold the tip to the bottom edge.

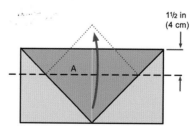

5. Fold the triangle part up along line A, as shown. The folding line should be about 1½ inches (4 centimeters) below the top edge.

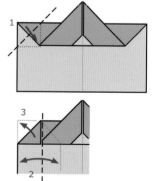

6. Three folding steps are marked in the figure. Fold the left corner as step 1. Crease along the vertical edge of the triangle flap as step 2. Unfold the triangle flap as step 3.

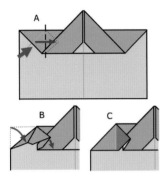

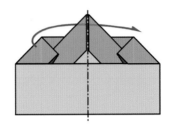

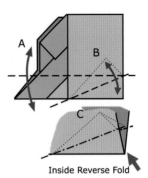

Inside Reverse Fold

7. Insert your index finger under the top layer of the corner and push to make a valley fold along the vertical crease, as shown in the three steps A, B, and C. The flap is made for a floating boat.

8. Repeat steps 6 and 7 for the right wing. Then fold the paper in half to make a mountain fold.

9. Crease two lines, as shown with arrow A and arrow B. Push the tail corner inward to make a tail fin, as shown in diagram C. It is an inside reverse fold.

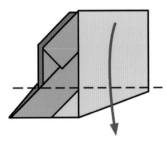

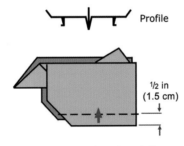

Profile

½ in (1.5 cm)

10. Fold the wing down.

11. Fold up the wing tips. Adjust the wings and the floats mounted on the wings to match the profile.

12. The Seaplane is completed. (Option: You may bend the tip of the float about 90 degrees to make a real float.)

SPYROS KONOFAOS

Hellenic Air Force Canadair CL-215 in flight (airpics.net)

The Canadair CL-215 is an amphibian turboprop airplane that is a flying boat with wheels. It is designed for forest-fire fighting. It can hold 1,176 gallons of water, and it refills its tanks by skimming the surface of any suitable body of water.

Mirage Fighter

The Mirage Fighter paper airplane resembles the Mirage 2000, a French-built fighter jet. The Mirage 2000 is a delta wing jet manufactured by Dassault Aviation, and it became a successful multirole airplane. It is now in service in nine countries, and more than six hundred Mirages have been built.

Like the Mirage 2000, this paper airplane has a long nose, which moves the center of gravity forward. To compensate for this effect, the elevators should be bent up sufficiently. It is a great-looking, excellent flier. It works best with fast launching rather than a gentle toss.

Folding Instructions

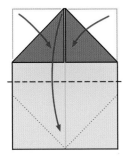

1. Crease lengthwise the center of a letter-size or an A4 sheet of paper. Fold the top corners to the center line. Bring the tip to the bottom edge.

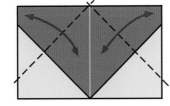

2. Fold the top corners inward to the center line, crease, and unfold. You may repeat with mountain folds for better creases.

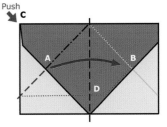

3. Fold the left top layer to the right side (A should meet B, and C should meet D).

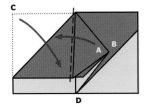

4. The top left corner has been pushed to center line D. Turn the triangle flap to the left.

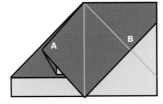

5. This is the result of steps 3 and 4. Repeat the same steps for the right-side corner. The result is shown in step 6.

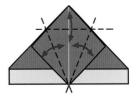

6. Crease the top layer as shown with three folding lines.

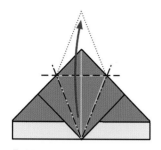

7. Fold up the top layer tip.

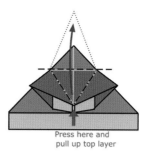

Press here and
pull up top layer

8. While pressing the bottom layer, pull up the top layer tip.

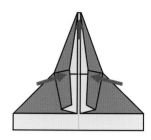

9. Pull up the tip and simultaneously fold the sides in.

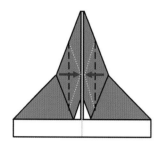

10. Fold both sides in to meet the center line.

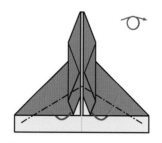

11. Mountain-fold the top layers as shown. Then turn over the model.

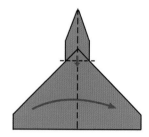

12. Fold down the tip of the top layer and fold the model in half.

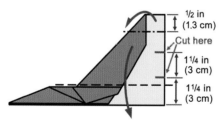

½ in (1.3 cm)

Cut here

1¼ in (3 cm)

1¼ in (3 cm)

13. Cut the elevators at the trailing edges. Fold down the wings and fold up the wing tips.

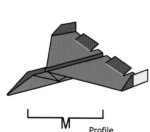

Profile

14. Adjust the creases of the plane to match the profile. Bend the elevator up. The plane is ready to fly.

French Air Force Mirage 2000 (flickr.com, July 19, 2010)

The tail-less delta wing of Dassault's Mirage 2000 became a favorable design for many modern high-speed airplanes. The delta wing gives a very high stall angle.

F-5 Freedom Fighter

The F-5 Freedom Fighter paper airplane has a very long, sharp nose and a double cockpit. The folding steps are very similar to the Mirage Fighter design until step 10, when the folding steps become quite different. The center of gravity of this plane is located very much near the nose, so this plane must have elevators to compensate. You may bend the trailing edge up or make your own elevators by cutting. Use double-sided tape to hold the two cockpits together. This is one of the best planes in this collection for flight accuracy and stability.

Folding Instructions

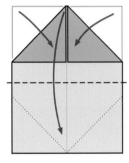

1. Crease lengthwise the center of a letter-size or an A4 sheet of paper. Fold the top corners to the center line. Bring the tip to the bottom edge.

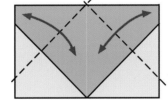

2. Fold the top corners inward to the center line, crease, and unfold. You may repeat with mountain folds for better creases.

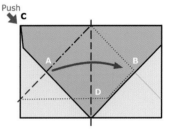

3. Fold the left top layer to the right side (A should meet B, and C should meet D).

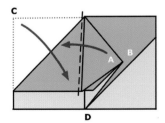

4. The top left corner has been pushed to center line D. Now turn the triangle flap to the left.

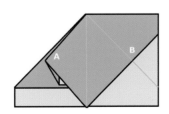

5. This is the result of steps 3 and 4. Repeat the same steps for the right-side corner. The result is shown in step 6.

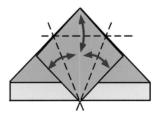

6. Crease the top layer as shown with three folding lines.

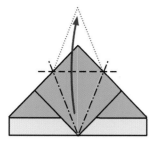

7. Fold up the top layer tip.

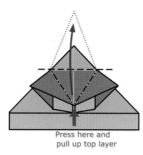

Press here and
pull up top layer

8. While pressing the bottom layer, pull up the top layer tip.

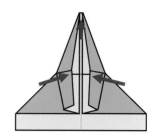

9. Pull up the tip and simultaneously fold the sides in.

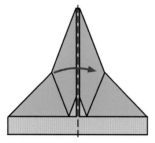

10. Fold the left-side flap to the right.

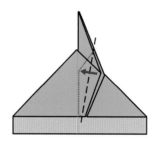

11. Fold the lower part of the flap to the center line.

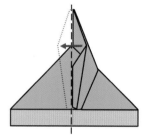

12. Fold the top layer to the left. Repeat steps 10 and 11 for the right-side flap.

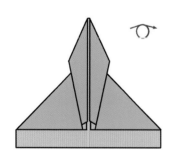

13. Now your model looks like this. Turn the model over.

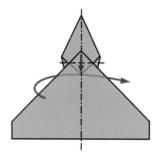

14. Fold the lower tip down. Then mountain-fold the model in half. Rotate the model.

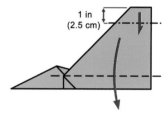

1 in
(2.5 cm)

15. Mountain-fold the wing tips. Fold the wings down. Note that the folding line is parallel to the bottom edge.

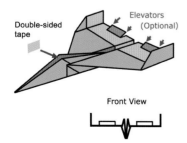

Double-sided tape

Elevators (Optional)

Front View

16. Use a piece of double-sided tape to hold both cockpits. Bend up the trailing edges or make elevators by your own design. The plane is ready to fly.

Northrop F-5E with AIM-9 Sidewinder missiles (National Museum of the US Air Force)

The F-5A/B Freedom Fighter and the F-5E/F Tiger II are part of a family of widely used light supersonic fighter aircraft designed and built by Northrop. Though less complex and advanced than some contemporary aircraft, such as the McDonnell Douglas F-4 Phantom II, the F-5 family was significantly cheaper to procure and operate, so it became a popular type of aircraft on the export market. The airplane had a compact size, high maneuverability, favorable flying qualities, a low accident rate, and a high sortie-generation rate. Similar to the Soviet Mikoyan-Gurevich MiG-21, many of the F-5s remained in service into the twenty-first century because of these positive qualities.

The F-5 was in service in the air forces of more than twenty-five nations as of November 2013.

Eurofighter Typhoon

The Eurofighter Typhoon paper airplane is designed to resemble the real Eurofighter Typhoon, which was developed by Europe's leading aerospace companies and is used by the air forces of seven nations: Germany, Italy, Spain, the United Kingdom, Austria, Saudi Arabia, and Oman. It is the most advanced twenty-first-century multirole fighter jet. The unique feature of the Eurofighter is the canard wings, or the small wings in front of the main wings. (*Canard* is French for "duck.") This paper airplane does not require any cutting or taping unless you use the optional elevators. Another option is to simply bend up the trailing edge. This plane is an excellent, cool-looking flyer.

Folding Instructions

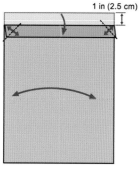

1. Fold the paper in half, crease, and unfold. Fold the top down along the line 1 inch below the edge. Fold both corners diagonally and then unfold.

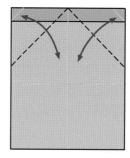

2. Fold both corners to the center line and crease. Then unfold.

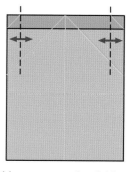

3. Fold, crease, and unfold as shown. The folding line starts from the intersection of the crease line and the top edge. It ends at the sloping crease line.

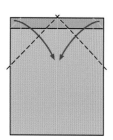

4. Fold both top corners to the center line again.

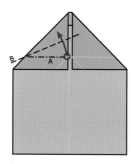

5. Fold the left flap along line B so that crease line A meets the sloping edge.

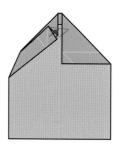

6. Bring a small triangle flap out of the mountain-folded part.

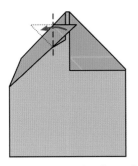

7. Fold the triangle shape flap to the left. Repeat steps 5 and 6 for the right side.

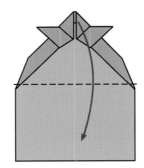

8. Fold down the paper so that the tip meets the bottom edge.

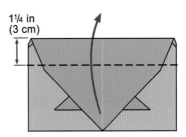

9. Fold up the top layer along the line 1¼ inches (3 centimeters) below the top edge.

1¼ in (3 cm)

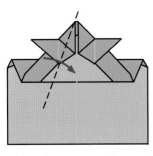

10. Bring the sloping edge to the center line and crease only the upper part.

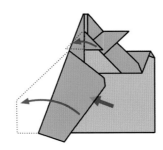

11. Place a finger under the flap and push out the flap to make a wing.

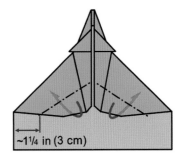

12. Repeat steps 10 and 11 for the right side. Mountain-fold and insert flaps under the layer.

~1¼ in (3 cm)

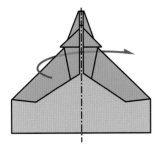

13. Mountain-fold the paper in half.

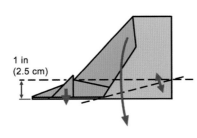

14. Bring the canard (the front wing) and the main wing down. Crease the tail part along the sloping line as shown. This part will become the tail fin.

1 in (2.5 cm)

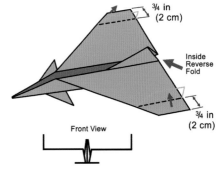

¾ in (2 cm)

Inside Reverse Fold

¾ in (2 cm)

Front View

15. Fold up both wing tips. Make an inside reverse fold to make a tail fin. Adjust the creases to match the front-view profile. Bend up the trailing edges or make elevators by your own design. The plane is ready to fly.

67

GEOFFREY LEE—PLANEFOCUS LTD.

Two Eurofighter Typhoons (Eurofighter Jagdflugzeug GmbH)

The Eurofighter Typhoon is a twin-engine, canard-delta wing, multirole fighter. The Typhoon was designed and is manufactured by Eurofighter Jagdflugzeug GmbH, which is made up of the major aerospace companies from the United Kingdom, Germany, Italy, and Spain. More than 460 Eurofighter Typhoon aircraft have been delivered to the seven countries that currently use this model.

F-4 Phantom Jet

The F-4 Phantom Jet paper airplane has jet-engine intakes that resemble the intakes of the twin-engine jet, the McDonald F-4 phantom. For the best results you may need to use a ruler and a pencil to draw accurate lines before beginning to fold. Having accurate folding lines is the key to this paper airplane. The origami version of this plane flies very well, and the second variation, with a few cuts, makes this plane look like the real Phantom Jet.

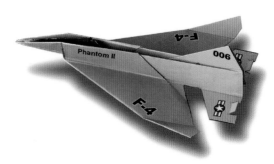

Folding Instructions

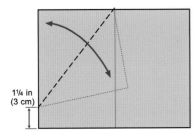

1. Fold the paper in half cross-wise and unfold. Then use a ruler to measure the folding line, as shown. Crease or draw the line with a pencil.

1¼ in (3 cm)

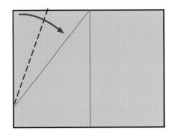

2. Fold the left edge to the sloped crease line.

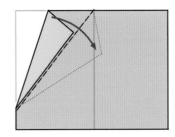

3. Fold the left edge again along the crease line made in step 1.

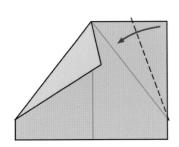

4. Repeat steps 1, 2, and 3 for the right side.

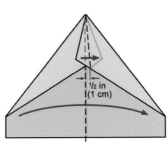

½ in (1 cm)

5. Fold the tip of the top layer as shown. This part becomes the canopy of the plane. Then fold the paper in half.

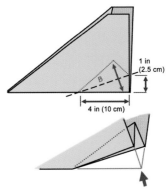

1 in (2.5 cm)

4 in (10 cm)

B

6. Use a ruler to make an accurate folding line B. Crease this line and make an inside reverse fold.

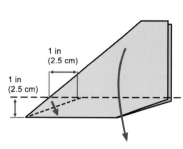

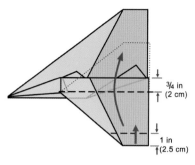

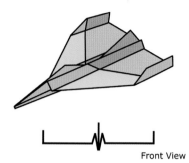

Front View

7. Use a ruler again to draw the folding lines as shown. Fold the nose part first and then the fold fuselage part. See the next diagram for how the engine intake part is formed.

8. Crease the wing tip as shown. Fold the wing up. Repeat steps 7 and 8 on the other wing.

9. Adjust the creases so that the model has the profile shown. The plane is ready to fly. If you want to use the scissors to make a more realistic Phantom Jet, go on to step 10.

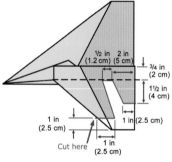

10. Open a wing and use a ruler and a pencil to draw a cutting line, as shown in red. Cut the red line on both layers together.

McDonnell Douglas F-4E Phantom II aircraft, Hellenic Air Force (airliners.net)

SVETLAN SIMOV—AVIATIONLISTONLINE.COM

The F-4 Phantom Jet is a twin-engine, all-weather, long-range, supersonic jet fighter originally developed for the US Navy by McDonnell Douglas. It was used extensively by the US Navy, the US Marine Corps, and the US Air Force during the Vietnam War. Beginning in 1959 it set fifteen world records for in-flight performance, including an absolute speed record and an absolute altitude record.

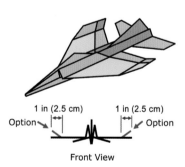

Front View

11. You may fold the wing tips as shown in the profile. The tail stabilizers can be slightly lowered, as on a real Phantom Jet. The plane is ready to fly.

Twin-Engine Airliner

This Twin-Engine Airliner paper airplane is inspired by the Boeing 737. Like the 737, this paper airplane has two engines under the wings. This design has two versions: a pure origami version, and one that requires a few cuts but more closely resembles the Boeing 737 airliner.

Folding Instructions

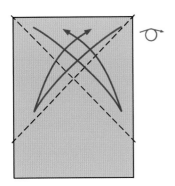

1. With the colored side face-down, make diagonal creases and unfold. Then flip the paper for the next step.

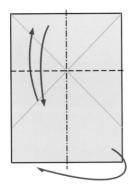

2. Fold down across the intersection of the diagonal creases and unfold. Mountain-fold the paper in half vertically.

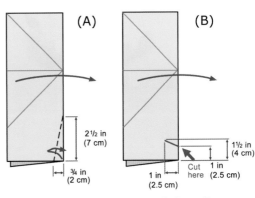

(A)   (B)

2½ in (7 cm)   ¾ in (2 cm)

1½ in (4 cm)   1 in (2.5 cm)   Cut here   1 in (2.5 cm)

3. Here we have two choices. For the origami version, make a crease as shown in diagram A. For the origami-plus-cut version, make a precut as shown in diagram B.

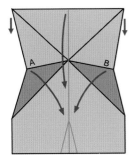

4. Lift both sides (A and B) and fold down to meet the center line. Collapse the top part to make a triangle shape.

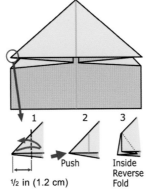

1   2   3
Push   Inside Reverse Fold
½ in (1.2 cm)

5. Fold the tip along the dashed line shown in diagram 1. Crease and unfold. Make an inside reverse fold by pushing the tip as shown in diagrams 2 and 3. Repeat for the right side.

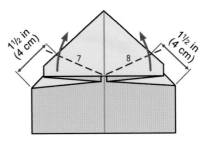

1½ in (4 cm)   7   8   1½ in (4 cm)

6. Fold both sides up along dashed lines 7 and 8 as shown in the diagram.

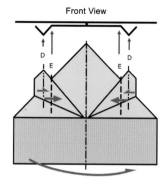

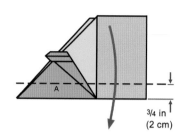

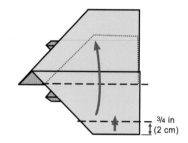

7. Valley-fold along line E and mountain-fold along line D. Adjust the creases so that the profile looks like the front-view diagram. Mountain-fold the model in half.

8. Fold the wing down along line A.

9. Fold the wing up along the edge of the fuselage and bend up the wing tip. Repeat steps 8 and 9 for the other wing. If you choose the origami-plus-cut version, skip step 10 and go right to step 11 for extra cutting.

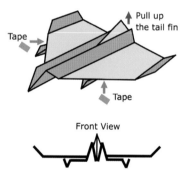

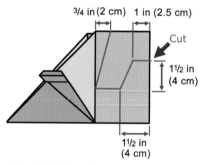

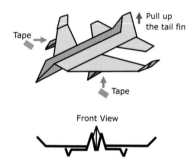

10. Pull out the tail fin and adjust the creases so that the model has the profile shown.

11. Unfold and go back to step 8. Draw a cutting line as shown in red. Cut away the upper corner parts and repeat steps 8 and 9.

12. Pull out the tail fin and adjust the creases so that the model has the profile shown. You may tape the engine sections under the wings for better flight. The Twin-Engine Airliner is ready to fly.

GEORGE MIHALEK

Boeing 737–800 aircraft (flickr.com)

The Boeing 737 twin-engine jet airliner is the most popular commercial passenger plane at this time. Each day, as of 2006, 4,000 Boeing 737s carry more than 1.3 million passengers; 1,250 of these aircraft are airborne at any given time, on average, and two are departing or landing somewhere every five seconds.

Twin Prop

The Twin Prop paper airplane has two overwing twin propellers. The folding steps to make twin propellers are a little difficult, but if you follow steps 5 through 7 carefully, you should be able to complete this sharp-looking plane. This design has two versions: a pure origami version, and one that requires a few cuts but more closely resembles the real plane with twin propellers.

Folding Instructions

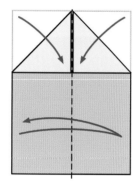

I. With the colored side face-down, fold the paper in half and unfold. Fold the top corners inward to the center crease line.

2. Fold the tip downward along the edge of the top layer, crease, and unfold. Turn the model over.

3. Fold the paper down along line 4. Then fold up the tip along line 3. (This crease line was made in step 2.)

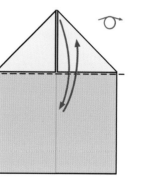
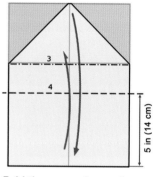

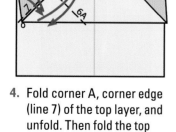

4. Fold corner A, corner edge (line 7) of the top layer, and unfold. Then fold the top layer of the section, labeled o, along line 6A. Unfold.

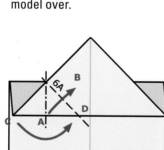

5. Fold flap A to B along line 6A while bringing flap C to D.

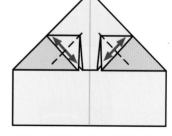

6. Repeat steps 4 and 5 for the right side. Fold the top layer corners outward. Unfold.

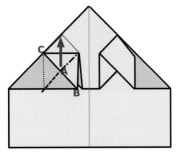

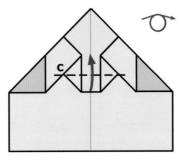

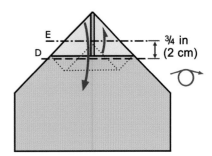

7. Lift A and fold upward while bringing B to C. Repeat on the right side. It should look like this.

8. Fold up the center flap along line C. Then turn over.

9. Fold the tip down along line D and fold the tip upward along line E. Then turn over.

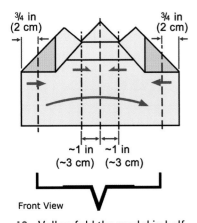

Front View

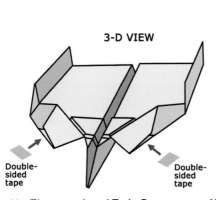

3-D VIEW

Double-sided tape

Double-sided tape

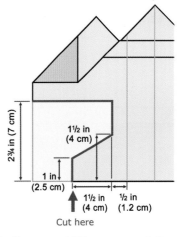

Cut here

10. Valley-fold the model in half. Then fold the wings down. Fold the rudders (wing tips) up. Note the front-view diagram.

11. The completed Twin Prop looks like this. You may insert a piece of double-sided tape into each propeller layer for better flight, and you may add elevators by cutting at the trailing edge by your own design.

12. If you would like more realistic twin props, go back to step 10 and cut the paper as indicated. Repeat step 11 for completion.

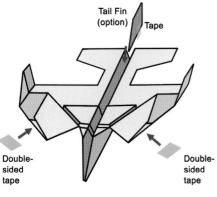

Tail Fin (option) Tape

Double-sided tape

Double-sided tape

13. The completed Twin Prop looks like a more realistic airplane. The plane is ready to fly.

Douglas C-47 Skytrain (US Air Force)

The Douglas C-47 Skytrain or Dakota (the British Royal Air Force designation) is a military transport aircraft developed from the civilian Douglas DC-3 airliner. It was used extensively by the Allies during World War II and remained in front-line service with various military operators through the 1950s. During the Berlin Airlift (1948–1949), Allied airplanes hauled tons of supplies for the citizens of West Berlin. The supply airplane took off or landed in Tempelhof Airport, West Berlin, every thirty seconds. The C-47 Skytrain played a major role during the beginning stage of the Berlin Airlift.

CHAPTER FOUR

ADVANCED DESIGNS

THE PAPER AIRPLANES in this chapter are the most advanced designs in this book. These designs try to resemble real airplanes as much as possible. There are more folding steps compared to the intermediate designs, but the folding techniques required for these planes should not be much harder. You will need to use tape and scissors for most of these advanced paper airplanes.

F-16 Falcon
Page 78

P-38 Lightning
Page 82

P-47 Thunderbolt
Page 84

U-2 Dragon Lady
Page 86

F-14 Tomcat
Page 89

P-51 Mustang
Page 93

F-22 Raptor
Page 96

F-15 Eagle
Page 99

F-16 Falcon Type 1

The F-16 Falcon paper airplane is my oldest design and has a swept wing with leading-edge extensions. Leading-edge extensions are often used with swept wings for modern fighter jets to improve flight performance at a high angle of attack. They are typically triangular in shape, with a line running forward from the leading edge of each wing root to a point near the cockpit along the fuselage. The Lockheed Martin F-16 Fighting Falcon is an example that has swept wings with leading-edge extensions. This paper plane is named the F-16 Falcon because it has the same characteristics. The original model is an origami version, and another version requires cutting and taping.

Folding Instructions

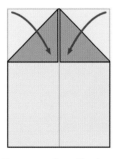

1. Fold the paper lengthwise and then unfold it. Fold the top corners inward to the center crease.

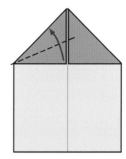

2. Fold the left top layer to the sloping edge as indicated by the arrows.

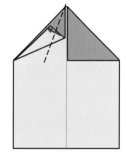

3. Fold the left top layer again, as shown. This part becomes the cockpit.

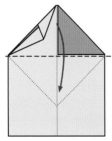

4. Fold the tip down along the edge of the triangle top layer.

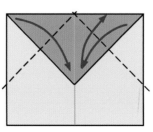

5. Fold the top corners inward to the center crease and unfold the right-side corner.

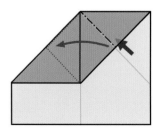

6. Put your index finger under the flap and lift the flap toward the left.

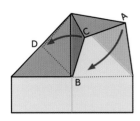

7. Flip the flap to the left side (so C meets D) and flatten point A to point B.

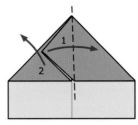

8. Fold this new triangle flap to the right side. Unfold the left-side flap and repeat steps 6 through 8.

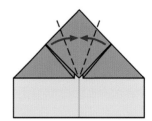

9. Fold both flaps toward the center crease.

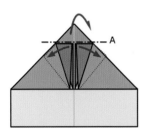

10. Make a mountain fold at the top corner section along line A. Unfold both flaps.

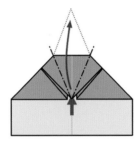

11. Put your index finger under the flap. Pull up the tip while pressing the base part.

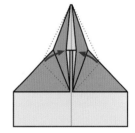

12. Fold the sides in and flatten the nose section.

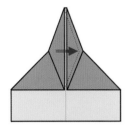

13. Pull out a triangle cockpit flap from the left side of the nose section.

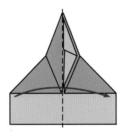

14. Fold the model in half.

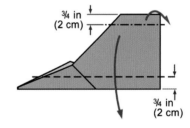

15. Fold the wing tips (a mountain fold) and fold down both wings. Keep the folding lines parallel.

¾ in (2 cm)

¾ in (2 cm)

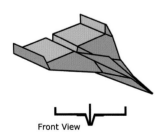

Front View

16. Adjust the creases to match the profile. Bend up the trailing edge of the wings for better lift.

F-16 Falcon Type 2

The variation is just an extension of the original model. Cutting is required to make the model resemble the Lockheed F-16 Falcon.

Folding Instructions

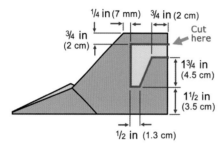

17. Steps 1 to 14 are the same as for type 1. Draw the cutting lines using a ruler and a pencil. Cut the red lines (both wings together).

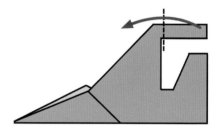

18. Fold the wing-tip tail to the left.

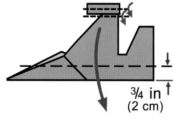

19. Fold the missile part in half and fold down one more time. Fold both wings down.

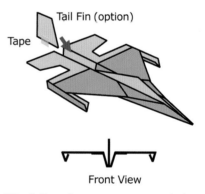

Front View

20. Adjust the creases to match the profile. You may cut a tail fin from another sheet of paper and tape it on the tail section. This is optional.

MASTER SERGEANT PAUL GORMAN

Four F-16C Fighting Falcons from the 115th Fighter Wing, Wisconsin Air National Guard, over Madison, Wisconsin, October 18, 2008. The leading aircraft has a unique tail flash that was designed to celebrate the unit's sixtieth anniversary. (US Air National Guard)

The F-16 Fighting Falcon was designed by General Dynamics in the early 1970s but is now a product of Lockheed Martin. The F-16 first flew in 1974, and more than four thousand have been built. Production will continue until 2017. The operators of the F-16 Fighting Falcon are Bahrain, Belgium, Denmark, Egypt, Greece, Indonesia, Israel, the Netherlands, Norway, Pakistan, Portugal, Singapore, South Korea, Thailand, Turkey, the United States, and Venezuela.

The F-16 design features cropped delta wings with leading-edge root extension and chin intake for the single engine.

P-38 Lightning

The P-38 Lightning paper airplane design is inspired by the real P-38 Lightning fighter, one of the most famous combat planes of World War II. The twin-boomed P-38 was the fastest American fighter plane in 1941. The paper airplane design requires a few cuts after folding. Its flight performance is excellent. It is somewhat difficult to adjust the thick creases to get the desired profile, but it can be done easily with the help of some cellophane tape.

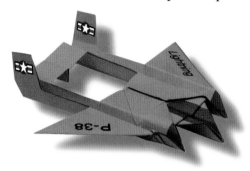

Folding Instructions

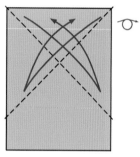

I. Make diagonal creases and unfold. Flip the paper over.

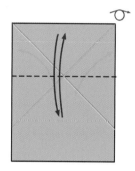

2. Fold down across the intersection of the diagonal creases and unfold. Then flip over again.

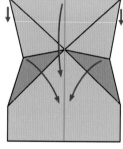

3. Lift both sides and fold down to the center crease. Collapse the top part to make a triangle shape.

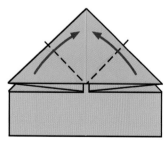

4. Fold each flap to meet the top corner.

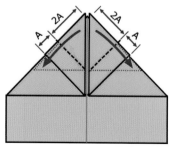

5. Fold down each flap along the diagonal line shown.

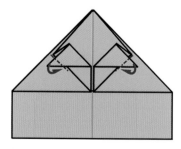

6. Mountain-fold the tips of the flaps and insert the tips under the diamond-shaped section.

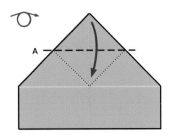

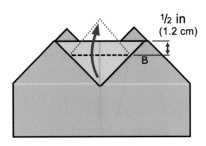

½ in
(1.2 cm)

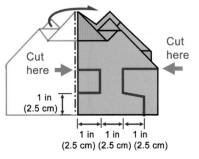

Cut
here

Cut
here

1 in
(2.5 cm)

1 in   1 in   1 in
(2.5 cm) (2.5 cm) (2.5 cm)

7. Turn the model over and fold the tip down along line A.

8. Fold the tip back upward along line B.

9. Mountain-fold the model in half, draw the red line, and cut along the line. Then unfold.

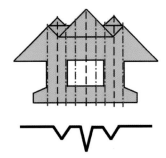

10. Make three valley folds (black lines) and six mountain folds (blue lines), then adjust the creases so that the model has a profile as shown.

Lockheed P-38J Yippee in flight (US Air Force)

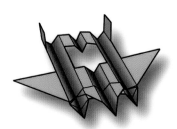

11. You now have a completed P-38 Lightning.

Developed to US Army Air Corps requirements, the Lockheed P-38 Lightning had distinctive twin booms and a single, central nacelle (enclosure) containing the cockpit and armament. This airplane was used in a number of different roles, including dive-bombing, level bombing, ground strafing, and photo reconnaissance missions, and it served extensively as a long-range escort fighter when equipped with drop tanks under its wings.

P-47 Thunderbolt

The P-47 Thunderbolt is a T-shaped paper airplane inspired by the American Republic P-47 Thunderbolt, a single-engine fighter during World War II. It was also known as the T-bolt. The tail fin and horizontal stabilizers on this paper airplane require accurate measurement and cutting in step 4. It is a great-looking plane and an excellent flier.

Folding Instructions

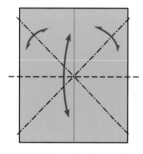

1. Fold in half vertically and unfold. Fold in half horizontally and unfold. Mountain-fold diagonally and unfold.

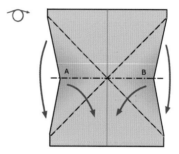

2. Flip over the paper. Lift both sides (A and B) and bring them to the center of the bottom edge. Collapse the top part to make a triangle shape.

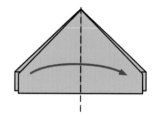

3. Fold the left top layer to the right side.

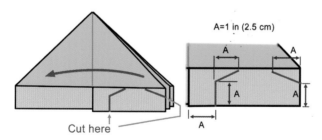

4. Use a ruler and a pencil to mark cutting lines, as shown. Then cut out two layers together along the red line. Fold the top layer back to the left.

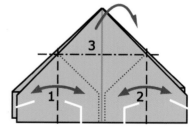

5. Fold both edges of the top layer to the center line along lines 1 and 2, crease, and unfold. Mountain-fold the top triangle along line 3.

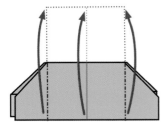

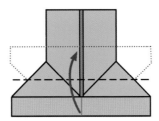

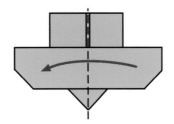

6. Put your index finger under the flap and pull up the top layer while pressing the base part. Bring both lower corners to the center line. Then flatten.

7. Fold up along the dashed line. This line crosses the midpoint of the sloping edge.

8. Fold the paper in half.

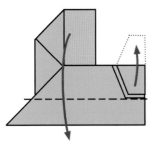

9. Pull up the tail wing. Then fold the wing downward.

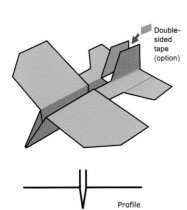

10. Pull up the tail rudders. You may use double-sided tape to hold the two rudders together. You may also use more tape between the wing and the fuselage.

Republic P-47N Thunderbolt (US Department of Defense)

The American Republic P-47 Thunderbolt was the largest single-engine fighter of its day. It was one of the main US fighter planes of World War II.

U-2 Dragon Lady

The U-2 Dragon Lady paper airplane has the long, narrow, straight wings and long fuselage nose of the actual Lockheed U-2 plane. Nicknamed Dragon Lady, the U-2 is a single-engine, high-altitude plane flown by the US Air Force and previously flown by the Central Intelligence Agency.

It can carry a variety of sensors and cameras for high-altitude surveillance. It was the U-2 that photographed the Soviet missile installations in Cuba during the Cuban Missile Crisis in October 1962. Just a few cuts are required on the paper plane. Double-sided tape may be helpful to keep the edge of the wings sharp.

Folding Instructions

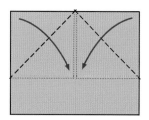

1. With the colored side facedown, fold the paper in half crosswise, crease, and unfold. Bring the top corners to the center crease line.

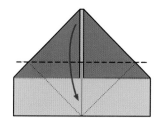

2. Fold the tip to the bottom edge.

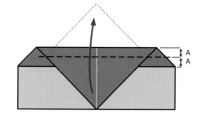

3. Fold the triangle part up along the line, as shown, and crease.

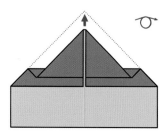

4. Pull up the triangle part and turn the paper over.

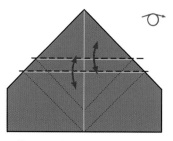

5. Repeat the same folding from steps 2, 3, and 4 for better creases. Then turn the paper over.

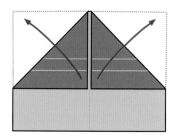

6. Open the folding.

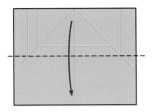

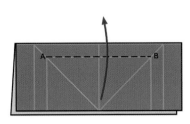

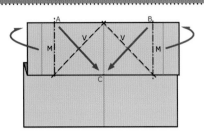

7. Fold the paper down in half.

8. Fold the top layer of the paper up along creased line AB.

9. Bring A and B on the top edge to C on the center line. This folding results in two valley folds along line V and two mountain folds along line M.

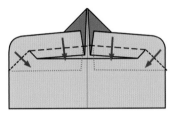

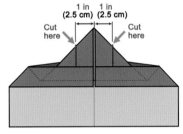

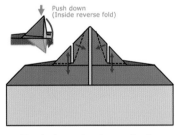

10. Fold down the top layer flaps as shown. The model should look like that shown in step 11.

11. Cut the nose part of the fuselage as indicated.

12. Push down both small triangle tips by using the inside reverse fold. Fold the nose part as shown.

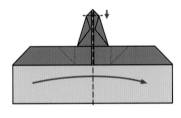

13. Fold the nose tip down. Fold the model in half.

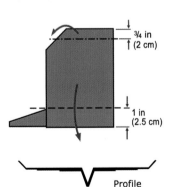

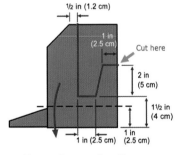

15. Draw the cutting line as shown. Cut the paper and fold down the wings. Adjust the creases to match the profile shown in step 14.

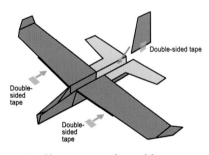

16. You may cut the rudder section and tape it to the tail. Use double-sided tape to hold the gaps at the front and the back edges of the wings. Now the plane is ready to fly.

14. Fold the wings down and bend the wing tips to match the profile. This is a version of the U-2 Dragon Lady. It is ready for launch. For the second version, go to step 15.

The U-2 Dragon Lady taxis to the runway at Osan Air Base, South Korea. (US Air Force)

The U-2 airplane has long glidelike wings. Essentially a jet-powered glider, the U-2 took off from a dolly, landed on skids, and could reach seventy thousand feet in altitude with a two-thousand-mile range. Most of the earliest U-2s were operated by the CIA before being passed on to the air force.

F-14 Tomcat

The F-14 Tomcat paper airplane is modeled on the Grumman F-14 Tomcat, a supersonic, twin-engine, two-seat, variable-sweep wing airplane. It has very special wings that can swing back for a higher speed and swing forward for a slower speed.

The paper airplane is also designed to have variable-sweep wings (also known as variable geometry wings). Cutting and taping is necessary for this model. The F-14 Tomcat paper airplane requires good accuracy during folding and cutting, but your attention will be well rewarded.

Folding Instructions (Unswept Wings)

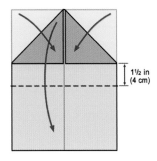

1. Fold the paper in half, crease, and unfold. Bring the top corners to the center crease line and fold down along the line, as shown.

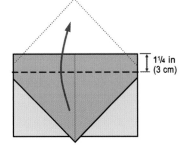

2. Fold up the top layer along the line as shown.

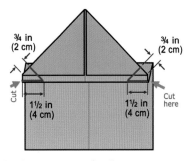

3. Accurate cutting is very important here. Use a ruler to mark the cutting lines, then cut out along the red lines.

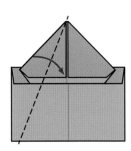

4. Bring the sloping edge to the center line. Crease only the upper part (see the next step's diagram).

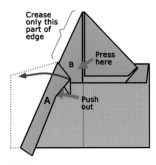

5. While pressing the B part, place a finger under A, push the flap outward, and flatten.

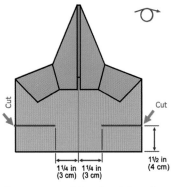

6. Repeat step 5 for the right wing. Make sure both wings have the same sweep angle. Cut the red lines and turn the paper over.

89

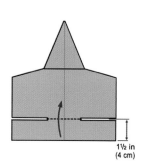

7. Fold up the tail part.

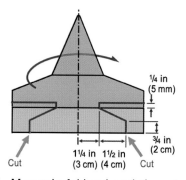

8. Mountain-fold and mark the cutting line with a ruler and a pencil. Then cut both layers together along the red line.

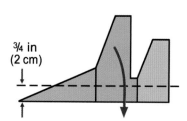

9. Fold both wings down.

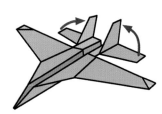

10. Fold up the tail fins.

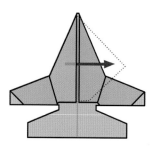

11. Open the model and pull out a triangle flap from under the layer.

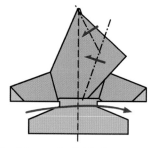

12. Mountain-fold along the sloping lines, as shown, to get the cockpit shape. Then fold the model in half.

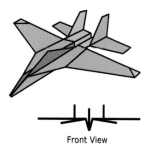

Front View

13. Adjust the creases until the model has this profile. Use a small piece of tape to make a flat wing layer. Your F-14 Tomcat is ready to fly.

Folding Instructions (Swept Wings)

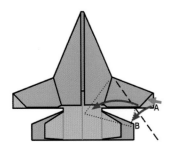

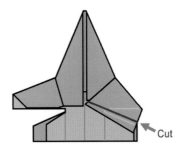

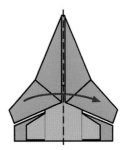

14. After you have completed steps 1 through 8, the model looks like this. Lift the top layer and bring wing tip A to point B. Flatten the layer.

15. Draw a red line parallel to the edge of the tail fin (keep about a ⅛ inch gap). Repeat for the left wing.

16. Go back to steps 11 and 12 for the cockpit design. Then fold the model in half.

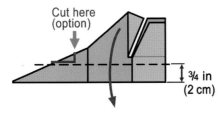

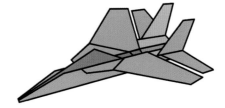

17. Fold down both wings. You may cut out a small triangle part at the shoulder. That resembles a jet engine inlet.

18. The completed F-14 Tomcat with the wings fully swept back should look like this.

F-14 Tomcat with wings unswept (US Navy)

F-14 Tomcat with wings fully swept (US Navy)

The Grumman F-14 Tomcat was the US Navy's primary maritime air superiority fighter and fleet defense interceptor beginning in 1974. It was retired from the active navy fleet in 2006, having been replaced by the F/A-18E/F Super Hornet.

P-51 Mustang

The P-51 Mustang paper airplane is modeled on the North American Aviation P-51 Mustang, a long-range, single-seat, single-engine fighter plane used in World War II and the Korean War. This paper airplane uses a fan-out folding technique to make the wings. It is a good idea to fold the F-14 Tomcat (see previous design) first before attempting to make this plane, since the fan-out folding is an extension of the technique used in that model. The P-51 Mustang flies very well and is good for outdoor stunts.

Folding Instructions

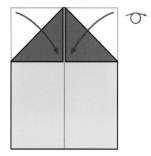

1. With the patterned side face-down, fold the paper in half, crease, and unfold. Fold the top corners inward to the center line. Then turn the paper over.

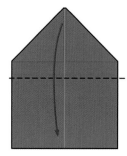

2. Bring the tip down to the bottom edge.

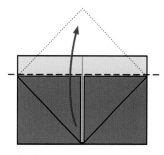

3. Fold the triangle section up.

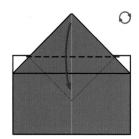

4. Fold the tip down along the top edge line. Rotate paper.

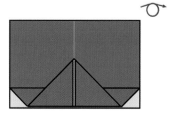

5. The model looks like this. Turn the paper over for the next step.

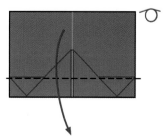

6. Fold down the top layer along the top edge of the lower layer. Then turn over.

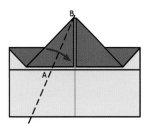

7. Bring the sloping edge to the center line and crease only the upper part (between A and B).

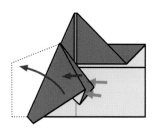

8. Now we have to do some tricky, fan-out folding. Bring the top layers to the left (red arrows) and simultaneously push out the folded paper. It is like opening a fan. Check the drawing in the next step—this is what we are aiming for in this fan-out folding.

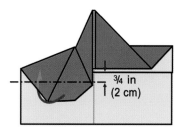

9. Mountain-fold the fan-shaped flap so that a horizontal straight edge is made. Repeat for the right wing, beginning with step 7.

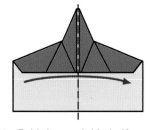

10. Fold the model in half. Choose either a mountain fold or a valley fold. The folding instructions in the next steps will assume you are using a valley fold. The photo image of the finished model, however, used the mountain fold in this step.

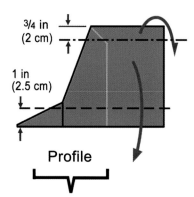

Profile

11. Fold the wing tips, fold down the wings, and adjust the creases to match the profile. This is an origami version of the P-51. To go further with cuts and tape, proceed to the next step.

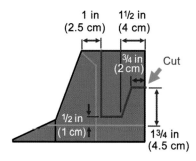

12. Draw the cutting line and cut the wings. Fold down the wings.

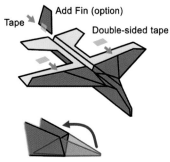

Inside Reverse Fold

13. Make an inside reverse fold on the nose tip. Use a piece of double-sided tape to make a flat wing. You may cut a tail fin however you like and tape it. The exact dimension is not important, and it is just an option. The Mustang is ready to fly.

GABOR HAJDUFI

North American P-51D Mustang in the Florida International Airshow in March 2014 (airliners.net)

The North American Aviation P-51 Mustang entered service with the Allied air forces in the middle years of World War II. In the Korean War it served as the main fighter plane of the United Nations Joint Command, but it was moved to a ground-attack role as jet fighters became more prevalent.

F-22 Raptor

The F-22 Raptor is a great-looking paper airplane made to resemble the Lockheed Martin/Boeing F-22 Raptor, which is the most outstanding fighter plane ever built. This paper airplane requires many steps and difficult folding. Although it is harder to make, it is certainly one of the most enjoyable paper airplanes you will fly.

Folding Instructions

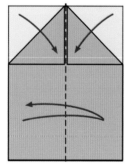

1. Fold the paper in half lengthwise and unfold. Fold the top corners to the center crease.

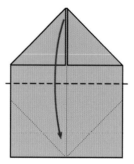

2. Fold down the top corner to the center at the bottom edge.

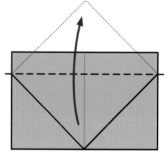

3. Fold the triangle section up.

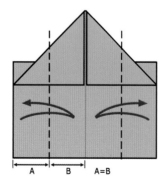

4. Fold both sides to the center line and unfold.

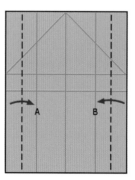

5. Unfold the paper completely. Fold the left side to crease line A, which was made in step 4. Likewise, fold the right side to crease line B.

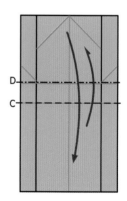

6. Fold the paper along crease line C, then mountain-fold along line D. The crease lines C and D were made in step 2 and step 3, respectively.

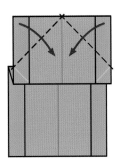

7. Fold both top corners to the center line.

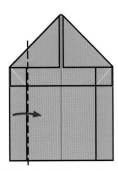

8. Fold the left side again along crease line A (shown in step 5).

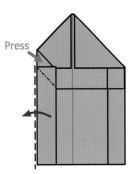

Press

9. Fold the left-side top layer toward the left while holding the top triangle part in place.

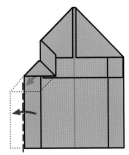

10. The folding in step 9 made another triangle pocket. Bring out the flap and fold the side top layer toward the left again.

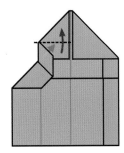

11. Fold up the lower part of the left triangle section. Part of the lower section should be pulled out from the diamond-shaped part, as shown with the green arrow.

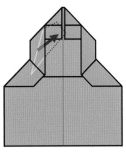

12. Repeat steps 9 through 11 for the right side. The model should look like this. Pull out the second layer from the shoulder part diagonally.

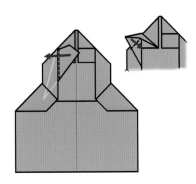

13. This flap becomes the cockpit. Fold this flap toward the left. Then fold it back to the right along the edge of the nose part.

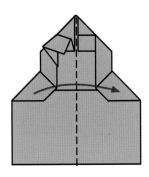

14. Now the cockpit is done. Fold the paper in half.

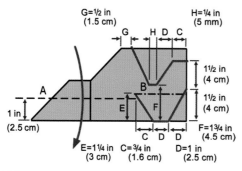

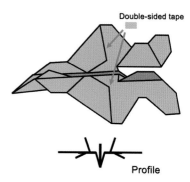

Profile

15. With a ruler and a pencil, draw the cutting lines as shown. The bottom line is for the vertical fins, and the top line is for the main wings and the tail wings. Cut out along the lines. Fold the wings down along line A. Mountain-fold along line B for the vertical fins. If you prefer an origami version of the F-22, skip the cutting and simply fold down the wings along line A. Go to step 17.

16. Adjust the creases until the model has this profile. Note that the vertical fins are slightly bent toward the outside and the tail wings are slightly lowered from the horizontal. You may use double-sided tape between the layers to hold the wings flat. The model is ready to fly.

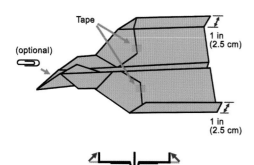

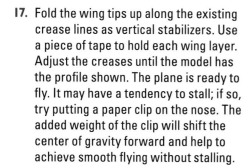

Profile

17. Fold the wing tips up along the existing crease lines as vertical stabilizers. Use a piece of tape to hold each wing layer. Adjust the creases until the model has the profile shown. The plane is ready to fly. It may have a tendency to stall; if so, try putting a paper clip on the nose. The added weight of the clip will shift the center of gravity forward and help to achieve smooth flying without stalling.

F-22A demonstration team performance during a 2009 open house, Holloman Air Force Base, New Mexico (US Air Force)

The F-22 Raptor fighter jet was developed to replace the US Air Force's F-15 Eagle. The F-22 Raptor is capable of maintaining a long-range cruise at supersonic speeds near Mach 1.5. This fighter jet is the leading American air-to-air fighter to date.

F-15 Eagle

The F-15 Eagle is a great origami paper airplane with twin vertical tail fins, closely resembling the actual F-15 Eagle fighter jet, an American twin-engine, all-weather tactical fighter designed by McDonnell Douglas. This origami airplane requires no cutting and taping, but it does require a special paper size. You will need a sheet of paper that is twice as long as it is wide (a 2 to 1 ratio). This unusual paper size provides extra weight in the front of the plane for better balance and pitch stability. The F-15 Eagle is one of the hardest paper airplanes to fold, but it is perhaps the most amazing plane in this book.

How to Prepare Paper with a Size Ratio of 2 to 1

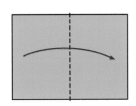
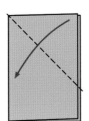
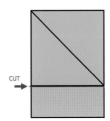

1. Fold the paper in half.

2. Bring the top corner to the side edge and flatten.

3. Cut the paper along the edge of the triangle flap.

Folding Instructions

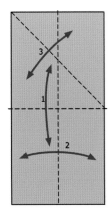
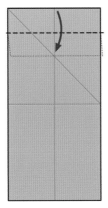
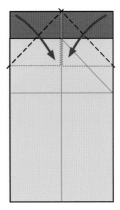

1. Fold the paper in half, crease, and unfold vertically and horizontally. Fold and unfold diagonally as shown in step 3's diagram.

2. Fold the top edge down to the crossing point of the center line and the diagonal line.

3. Fold the top corners inward to the center line.

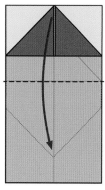

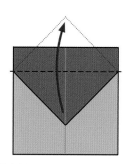

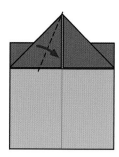

4. Fold the upper section down along the horizontal center line that was made in step 1.

5. Fold the triangle section up along the line, as shown.

6. Bring the sloping edge to the center line.

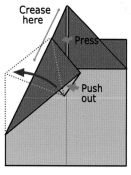

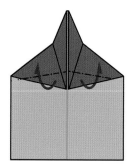

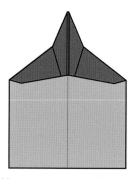

7. Crease the upper part of the sloping edge. While pressing the triangle part, place a finger under the flap, push outward, and flatten.

8. Repeat step 7 for the right side of the model. Then mountain-fold the flaps and tuck inside.

9. Your model should look like this.

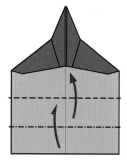

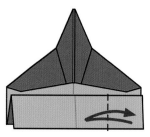

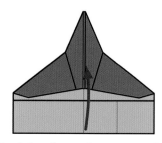

10. Divide the paper into three equal parts along the side edge. Mountain-fold and valley-fold as shown.

11. Bring the side edge to the center line, crease, and unfold.

12. Bring the top layer upward.

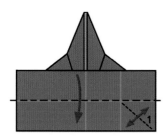

13. Fold along line 1 and unfold. Fold the top layer down.

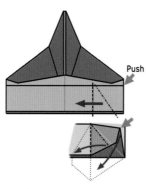

14. Push down the corner of the flap so that the valley and mountain folds can be done. Use line 1 (labeled in step 13) as a folding line for the second layer.

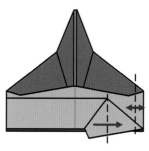

15. Fold the tail fin along the vertical line. Fold the wing tip as shown and unfold. Repeat the same folding for the other side.

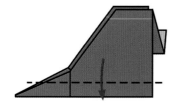

16. Fold the model in half. Open the wing section as shown.

17. Adjust the creases until the model has this shape. The optional canopy is included here.

Optional Canopy Folding Instructions

After step 3 the following steps may be included for the optional canopy design:

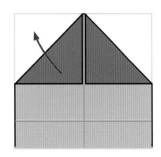

1. Open the left-side top layer.

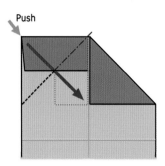

Push

2. Push the left-side corner to make an inside reverse fold.

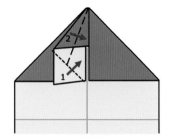

3. Make two valley folds, as shown, for the canopy.

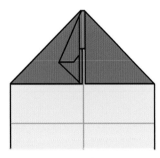

4. The canopy should look like this. You may keep the canopy upward for the next steps.

TECH. SGT. BEN BLOKER

F-15 Eagles flying over the nest during the final training mission of the 27th Fighter Squadron (US Air Force)

The F-15 Eagle is among the most successful modern fighters, with more than one hundred aerial combat victories. The Eagle first flew in July 1972 and entered service in 1976. It is expected to be in service with the US Air Force past 2025. Various F-15 versions are still being produced for foreign users, which include Israel, Saudi Arabia, Japan, and South Korea.

PAPER AIRPLANE TEMPLATES

FULL-COLOR TEMPLATES FOR all the paper airplane models are provided in this appendix. You are welcome to make photocopies and use them when you fold the planes. The templates will make it much easier for you to fold the paper airplanes, and the finished models will be much more attractive. The templates for all the airplanes in this book are also available on the Internet for you to download and print.

The website address for the templates is templates.amazingpaperairplanes.com.

Classic Dart

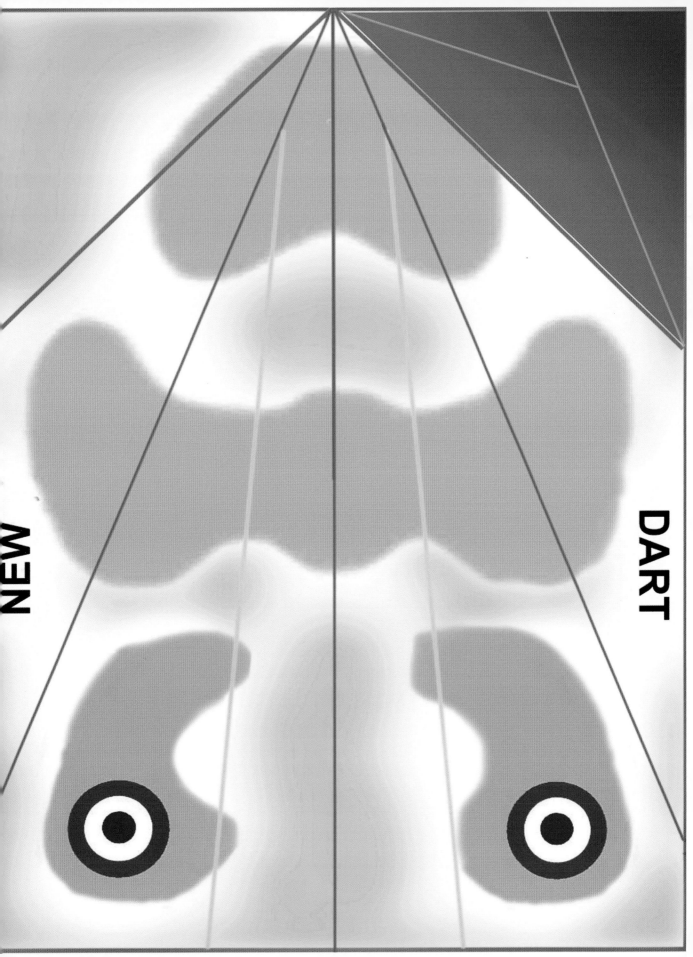

Classic Glider—Type 1

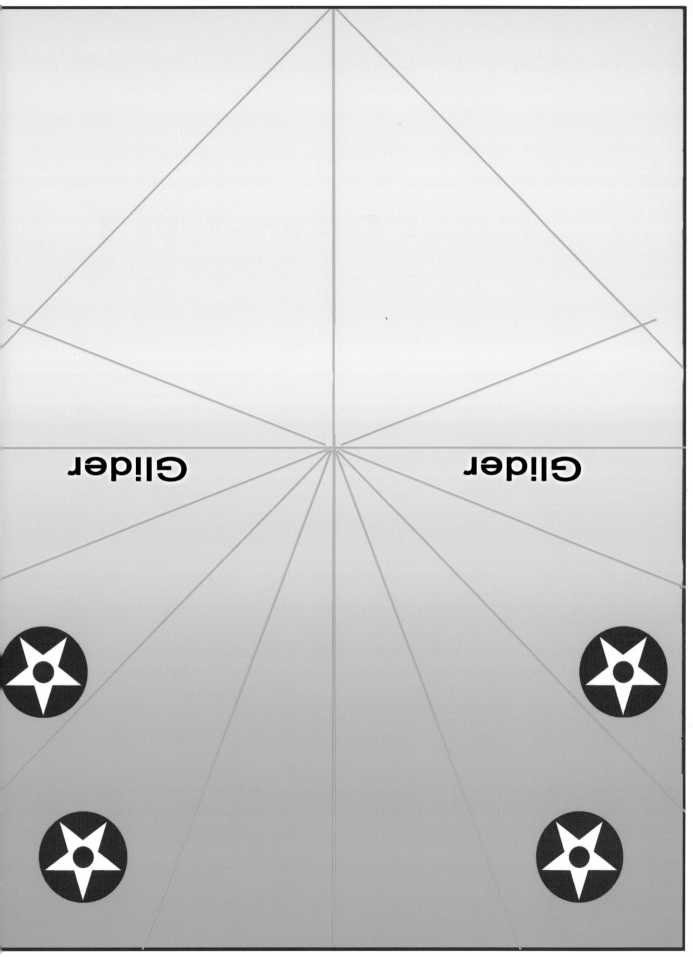

Classic Glider—Type 2

New Glider

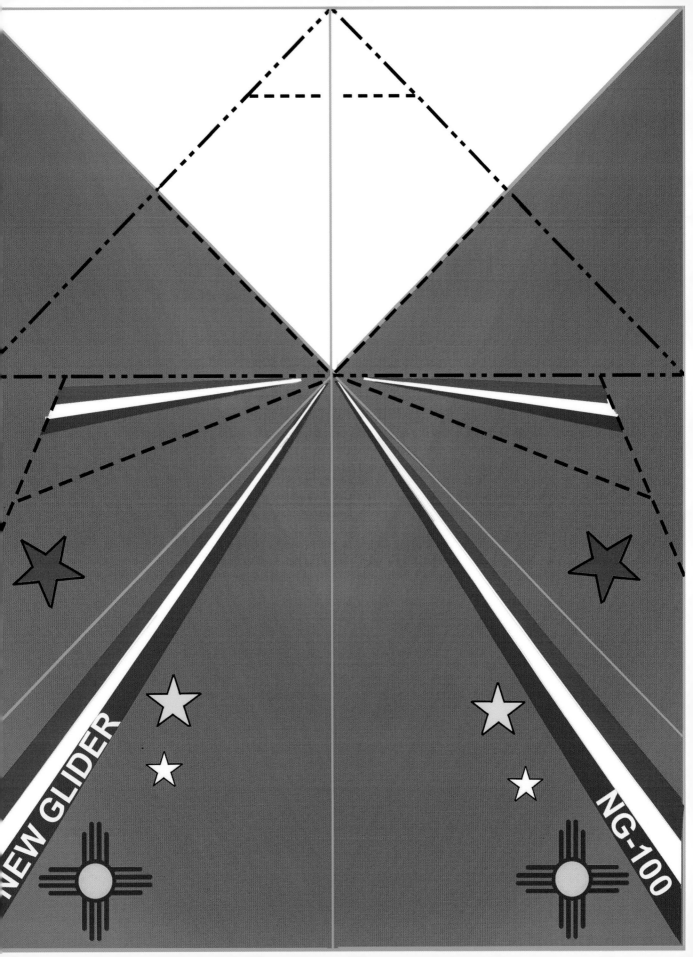

Flying Wing

FLYING

WING - F1

Square Wing

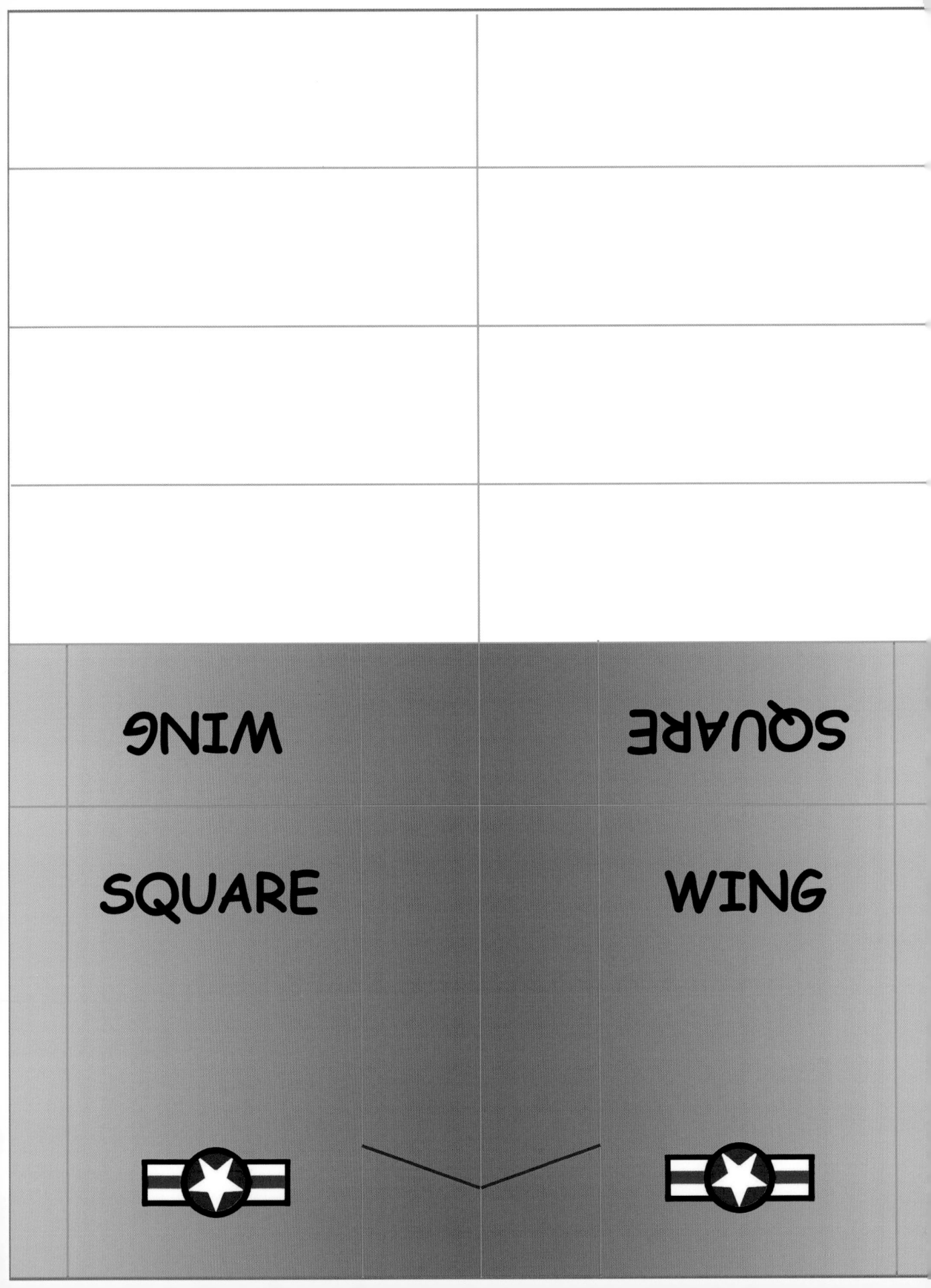

SQUARE

WING

WING

SQUARE

Wildcat Fighter—Type 1

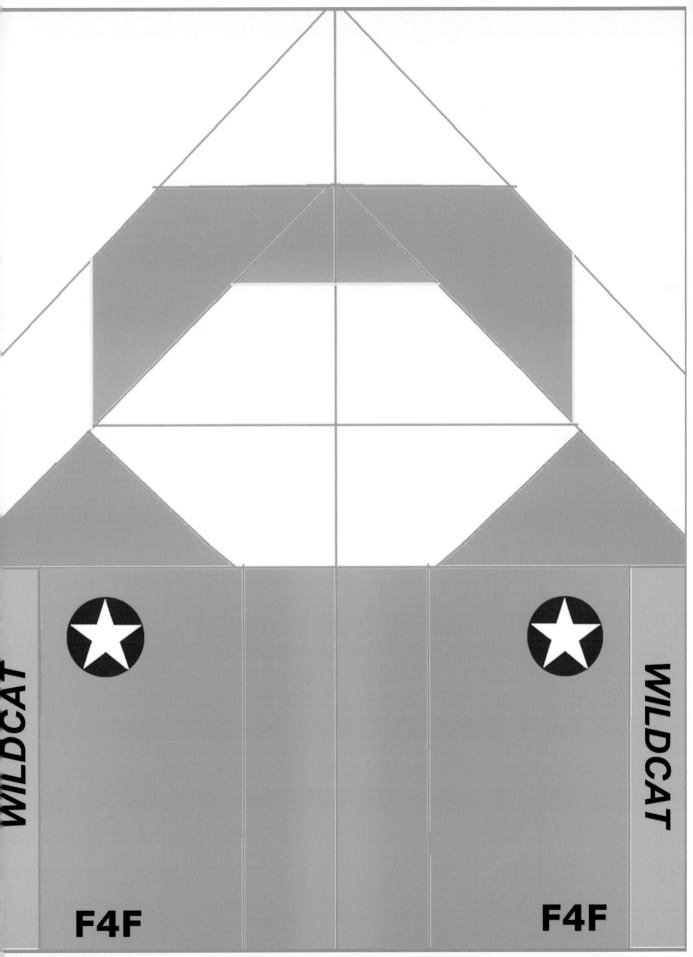

WILDCAT

WILDCAT

F4F

F4F

Wildcat Fighter—Type 2

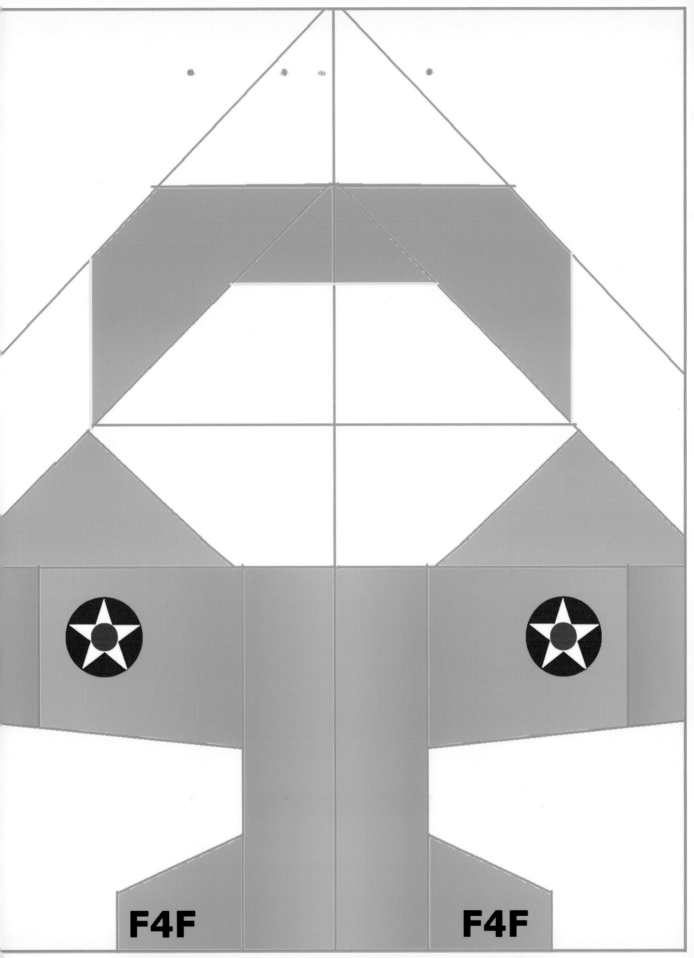

F4F

F4F

Delta Fighter

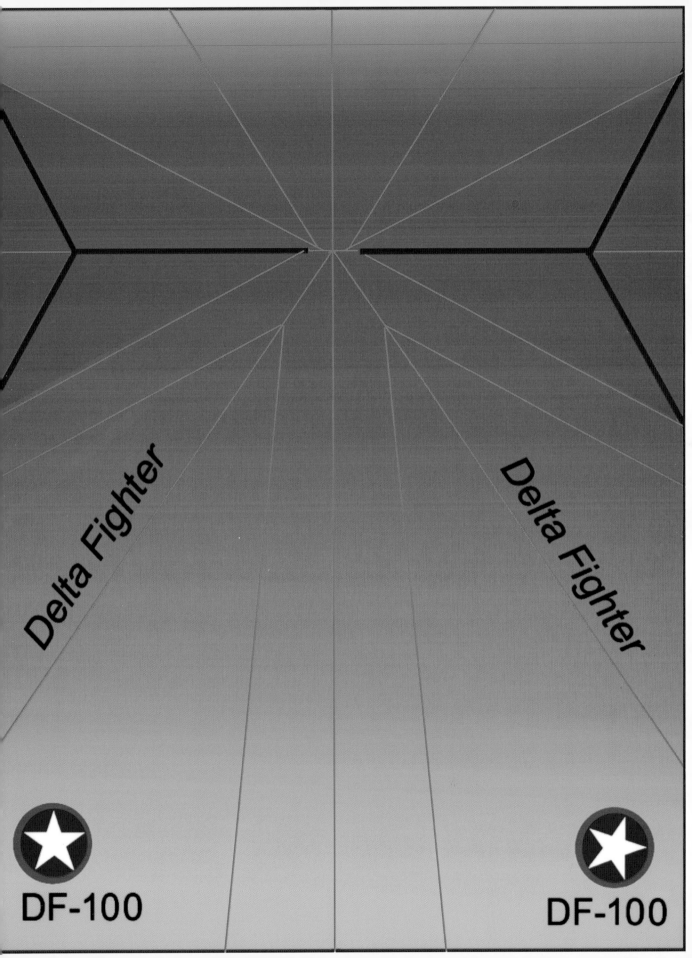

Space Shuttle—Type 1

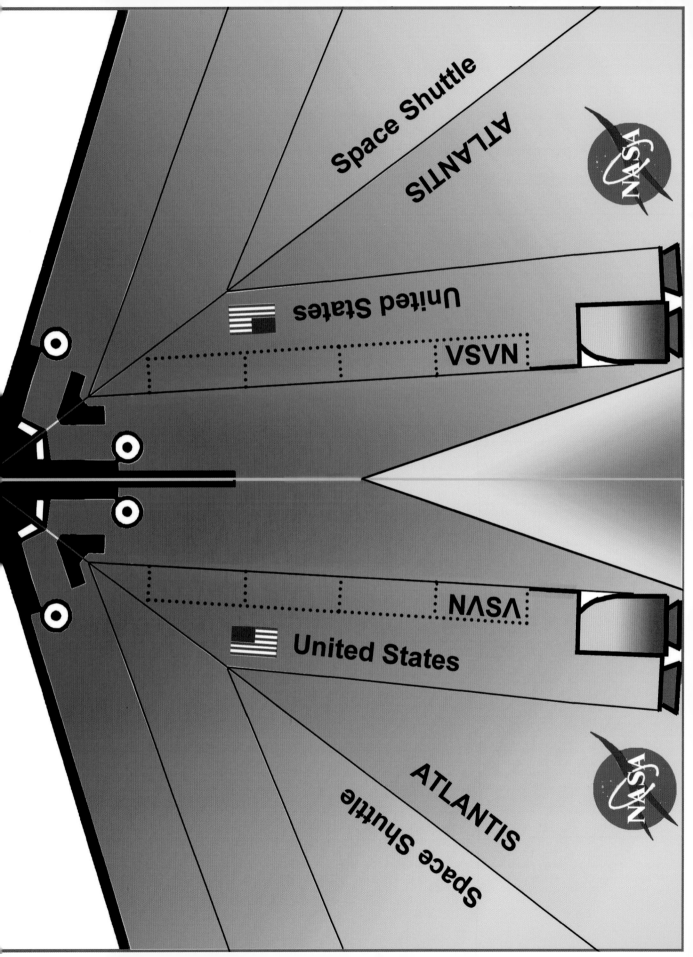

Space Shuttle—Type 2

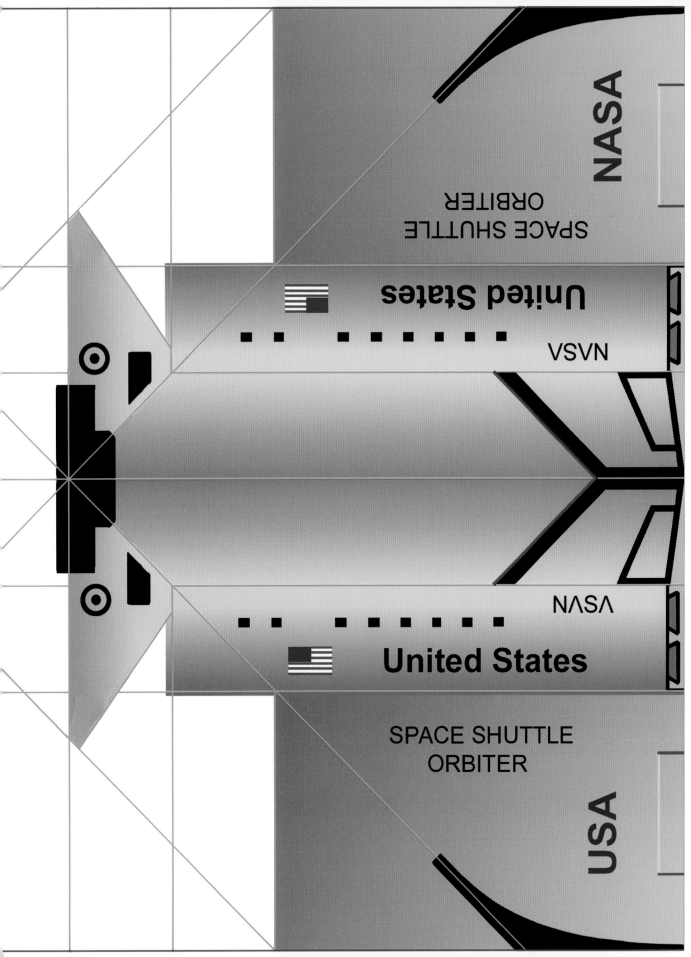

Twin Mustang

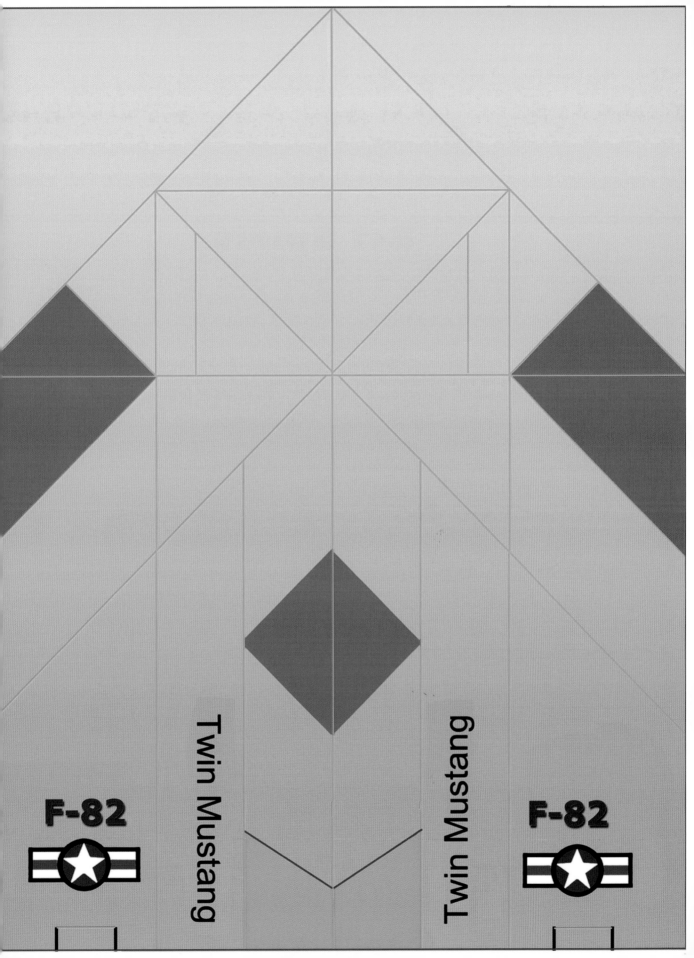

F-82

Twin Mustang

Twin Mustang

F-82

B-2 Spirit

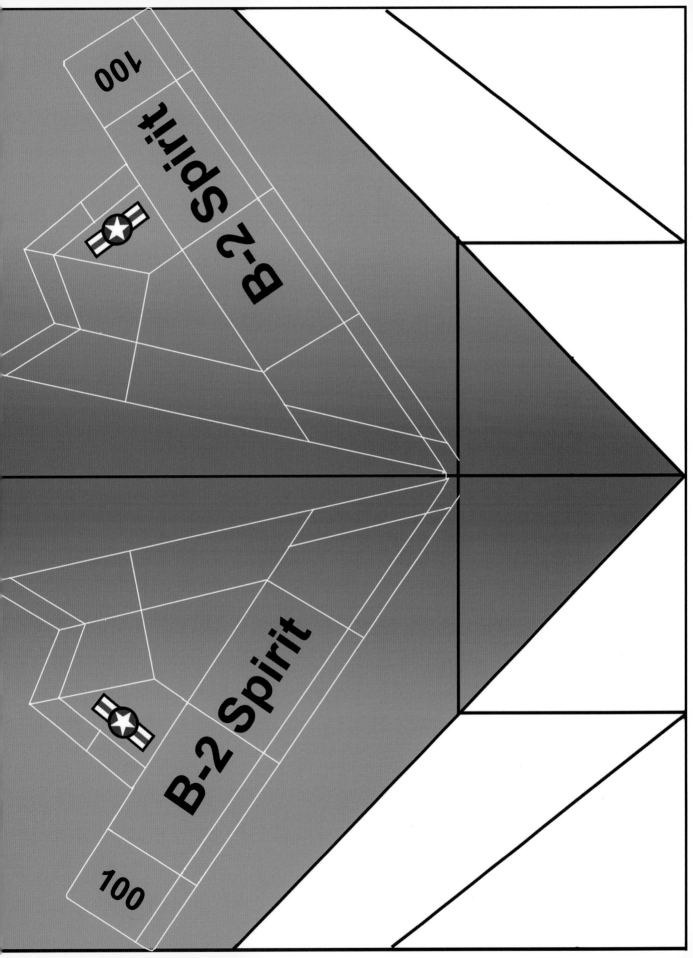

F-117 Nighthawk

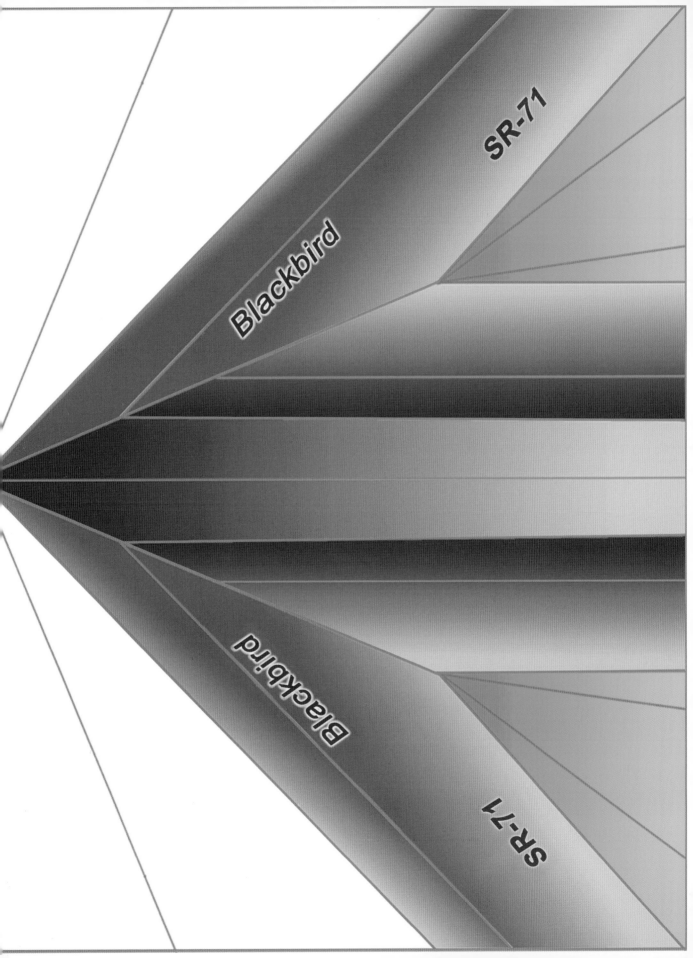

Twin Tailfin

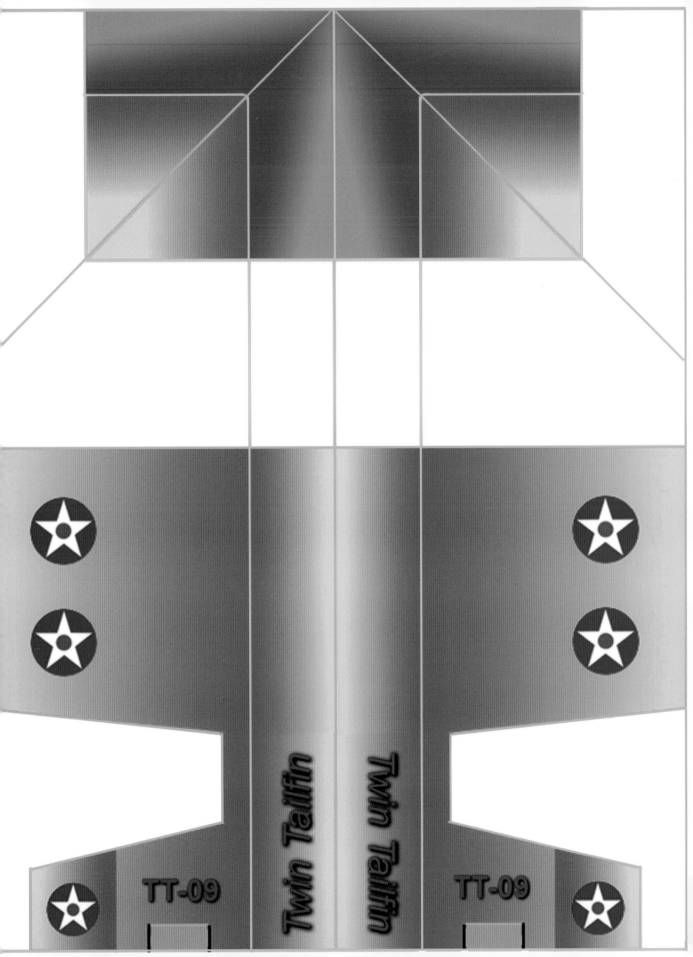

Twin Tailfin

Twin Tailfin

TT-09

TT-09

F-102 Delta Dagger

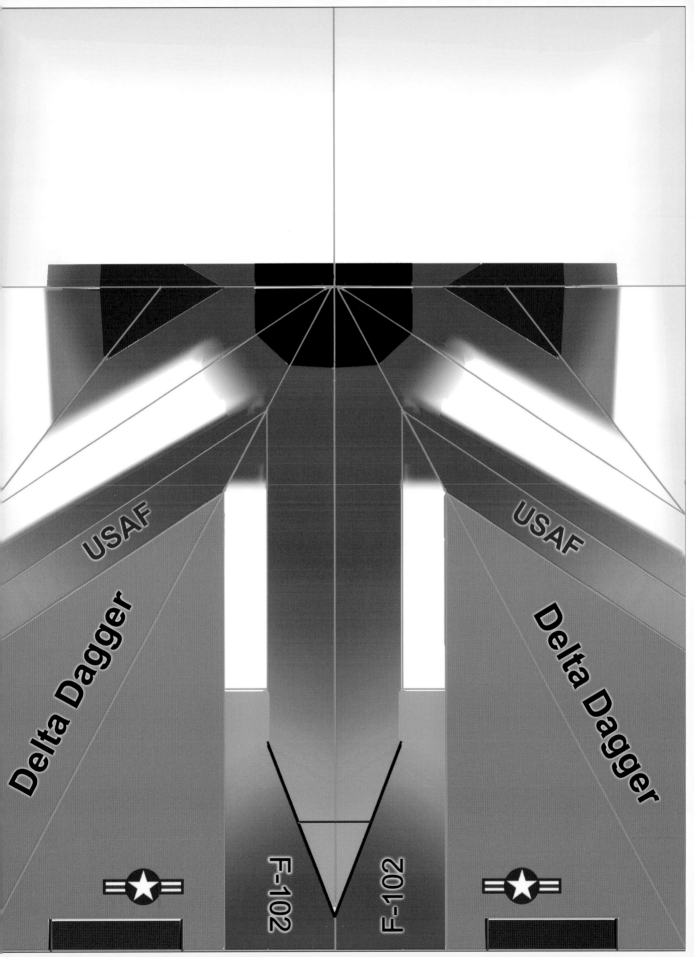

Concorde Airliner

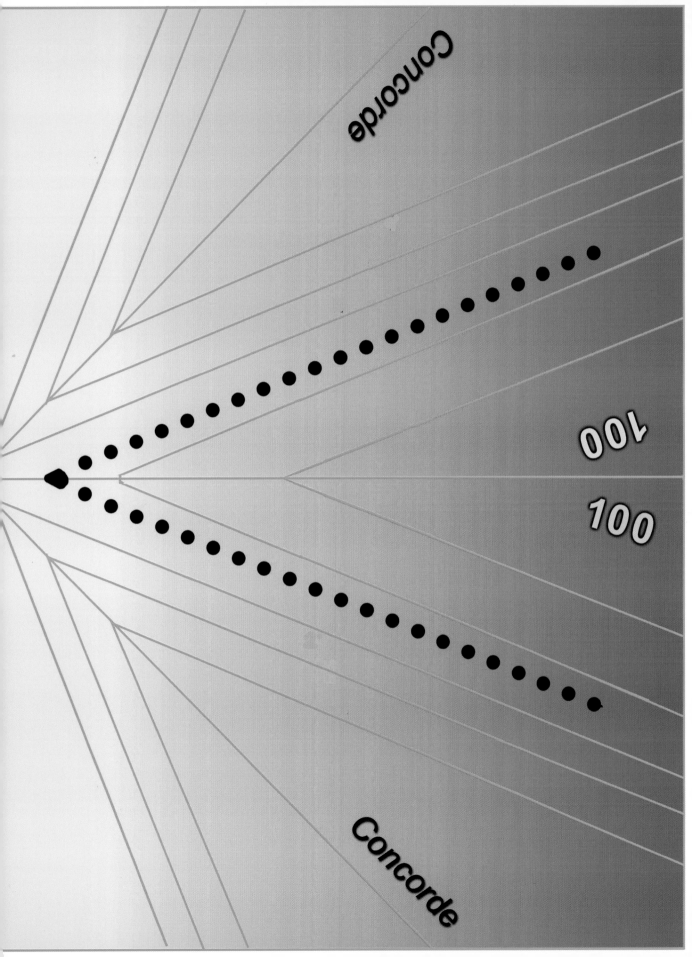

Seaplane

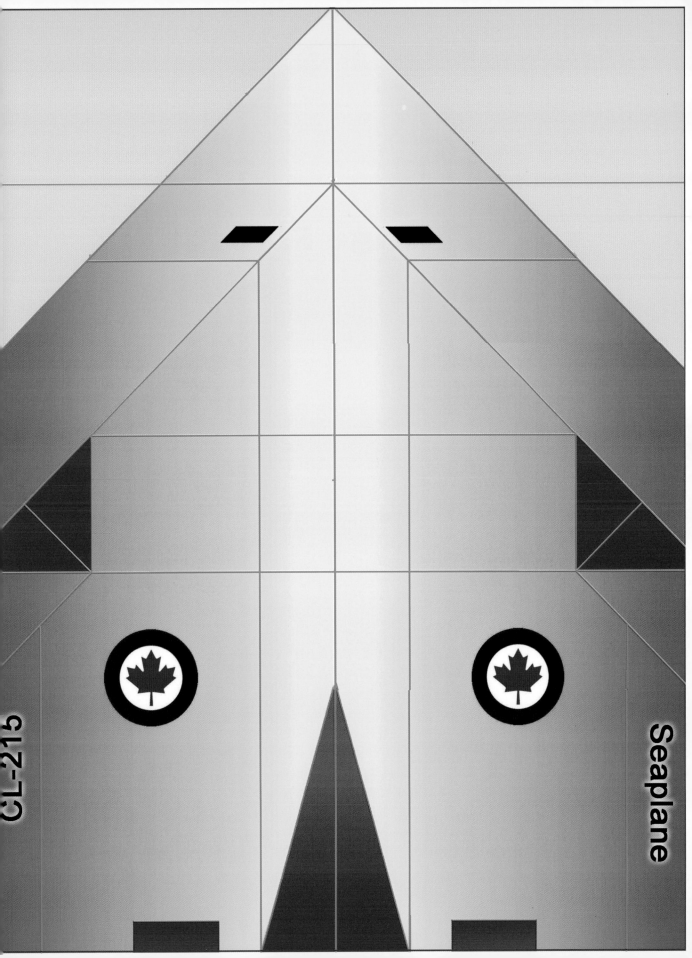

Mirage Fighter

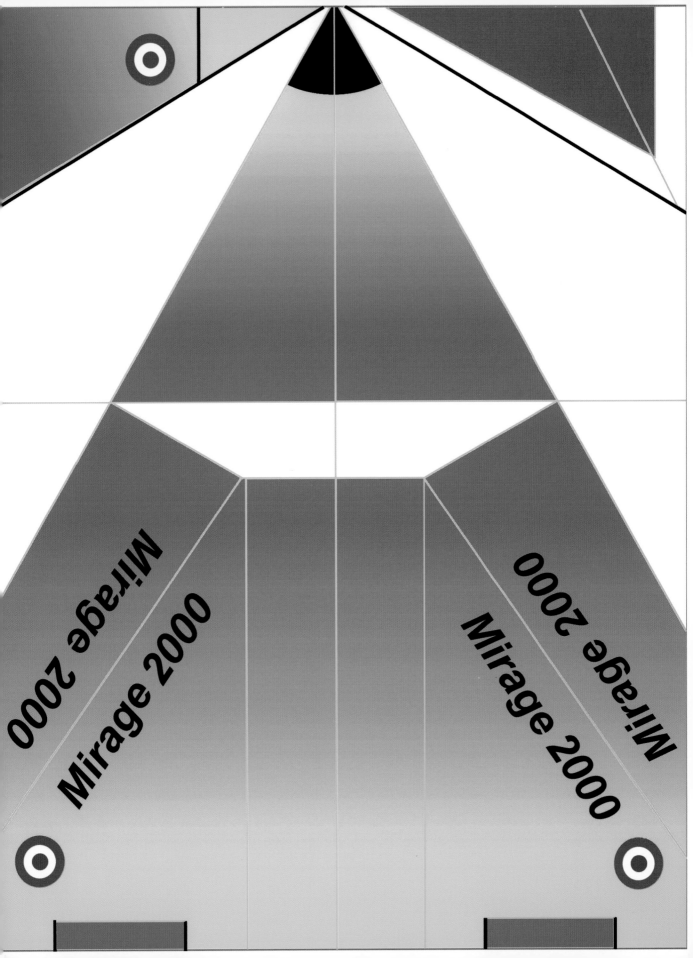

F-5 Freedom Fighter

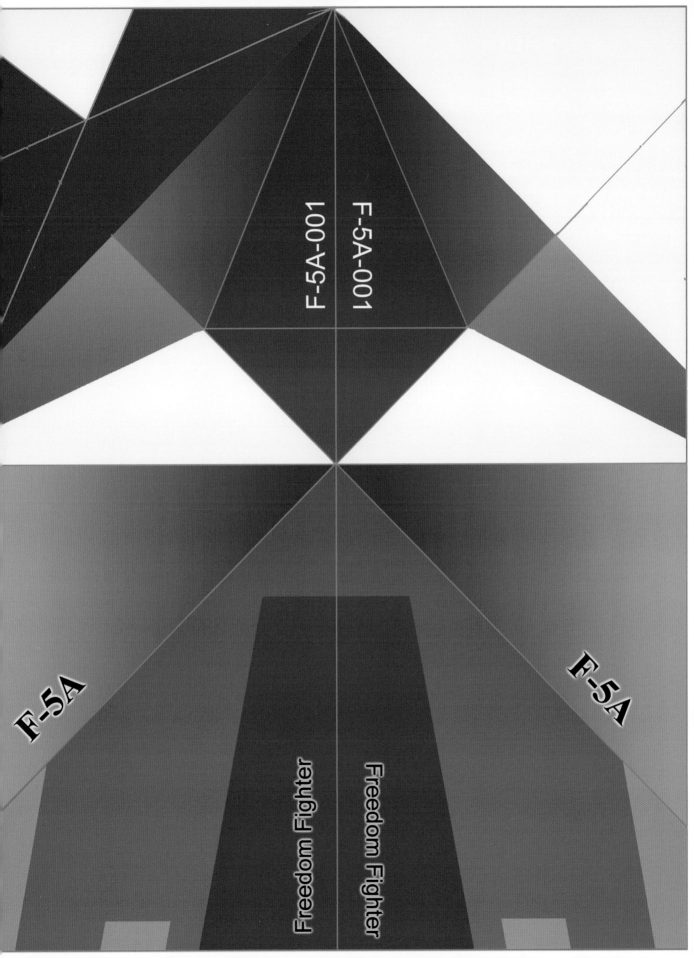

Eurofighter Typhoon

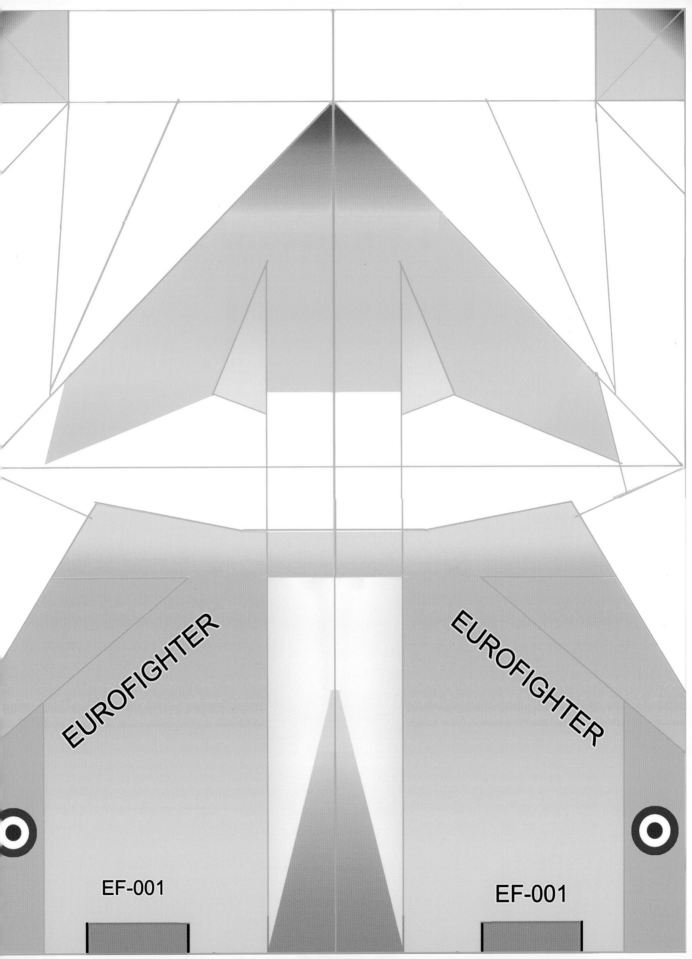

F-4 Phantom Jet

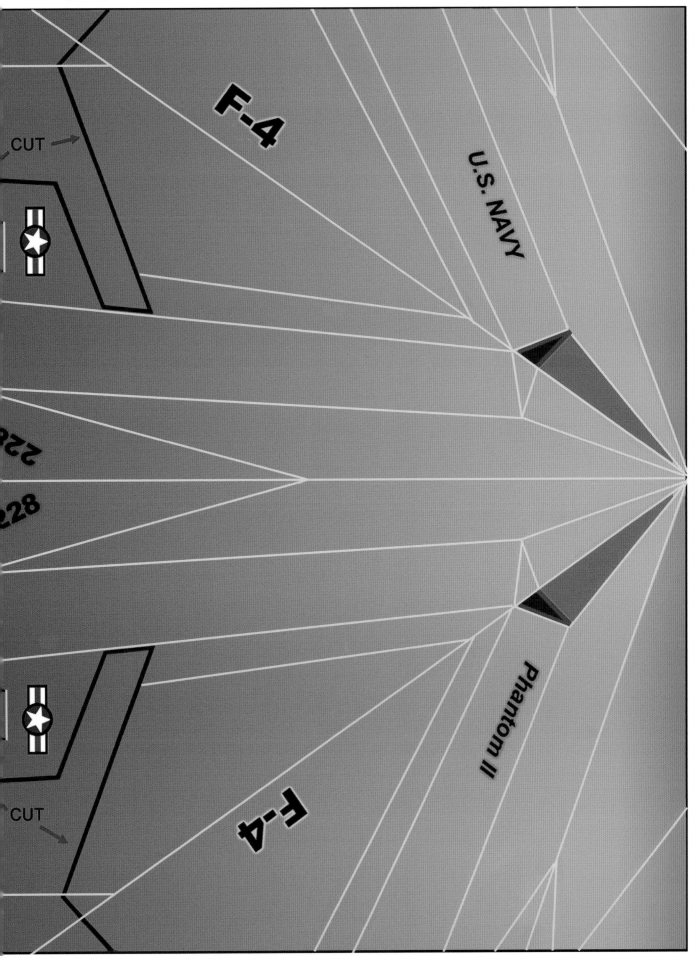

Twin-Engine Airliner

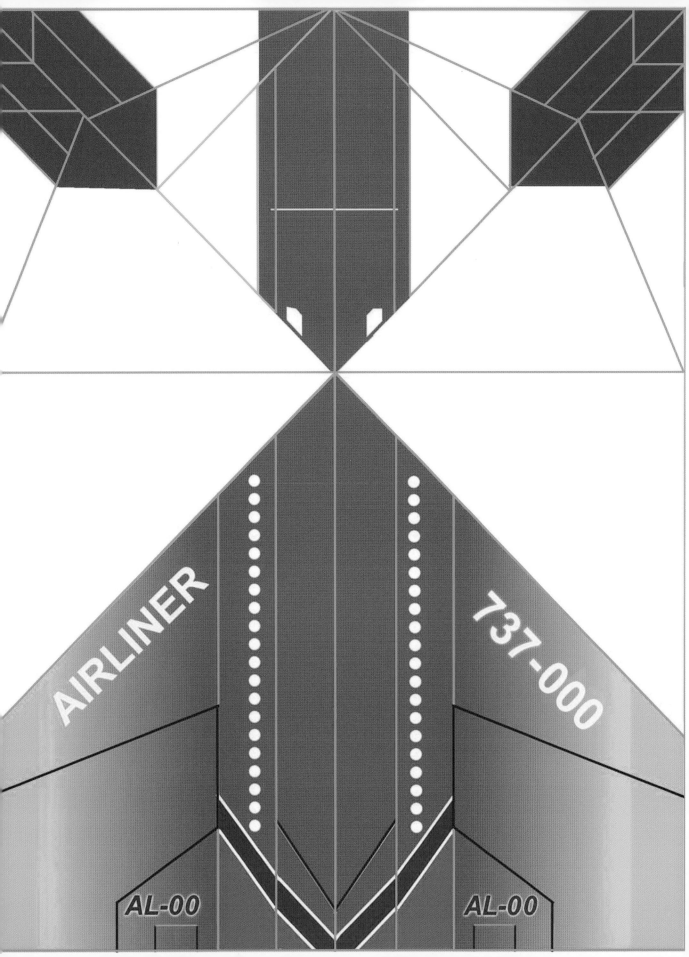

Twin Prop

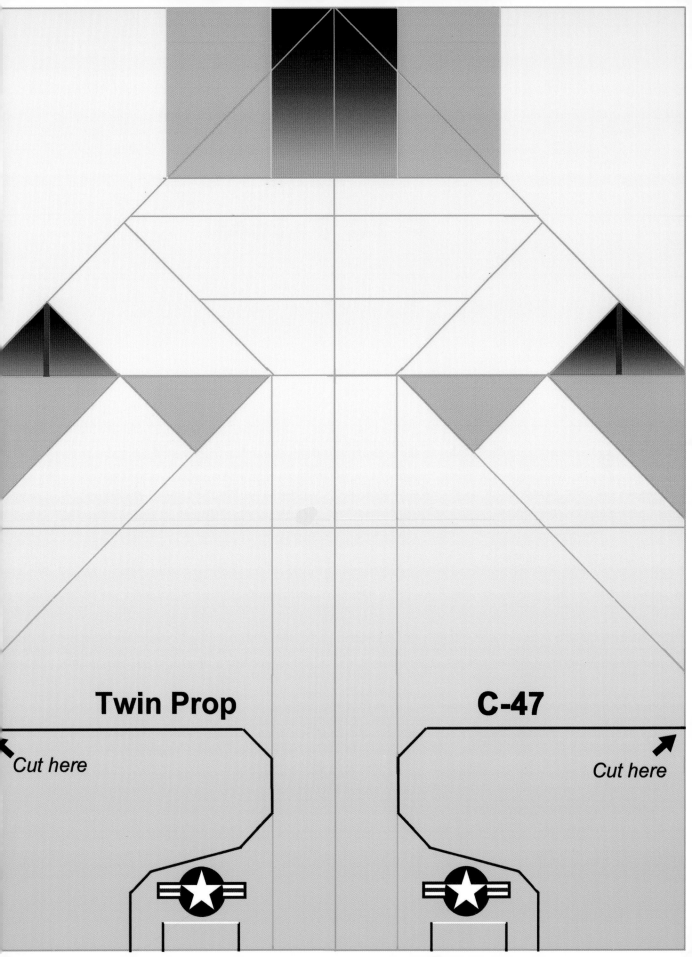

Twin Prop

Cut here

C-47

Cut here

F-16 Falcon

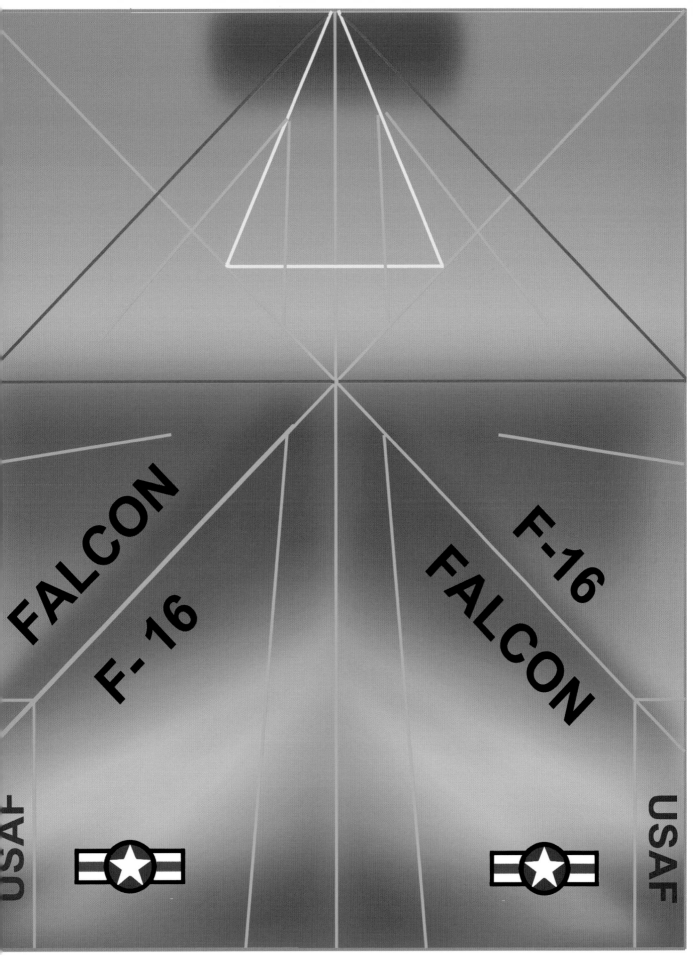

P-38 Lightning

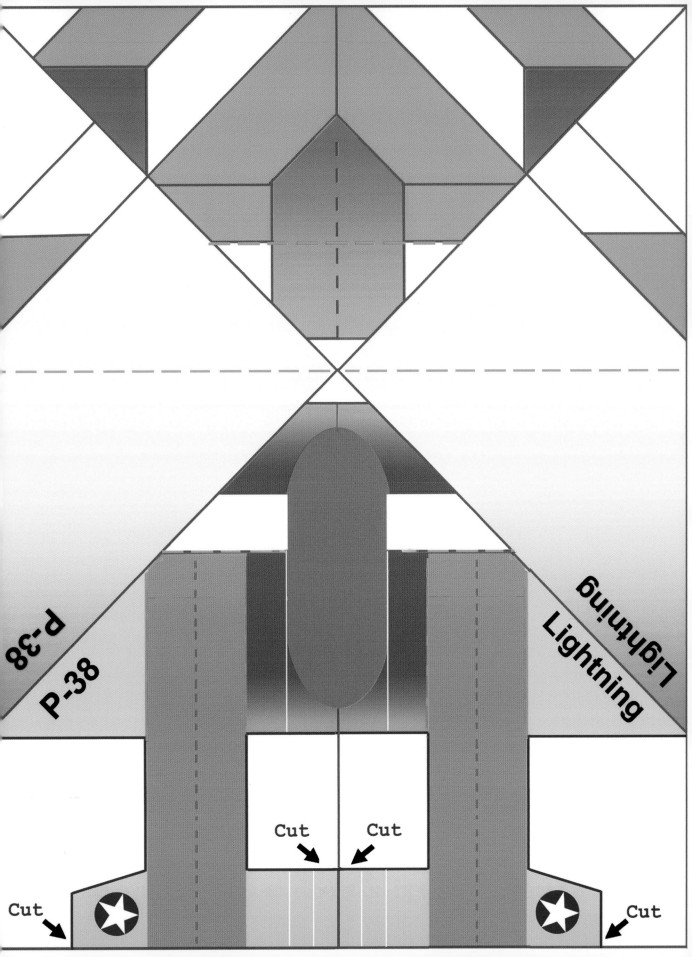

P-47 Thunderbolt

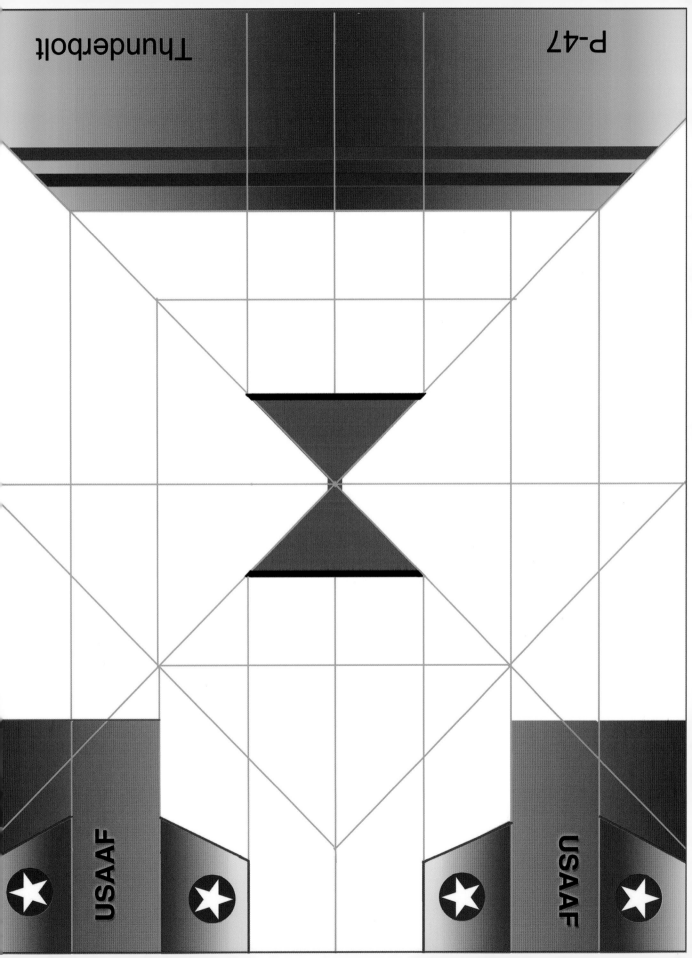

U-2 Dragon Lady

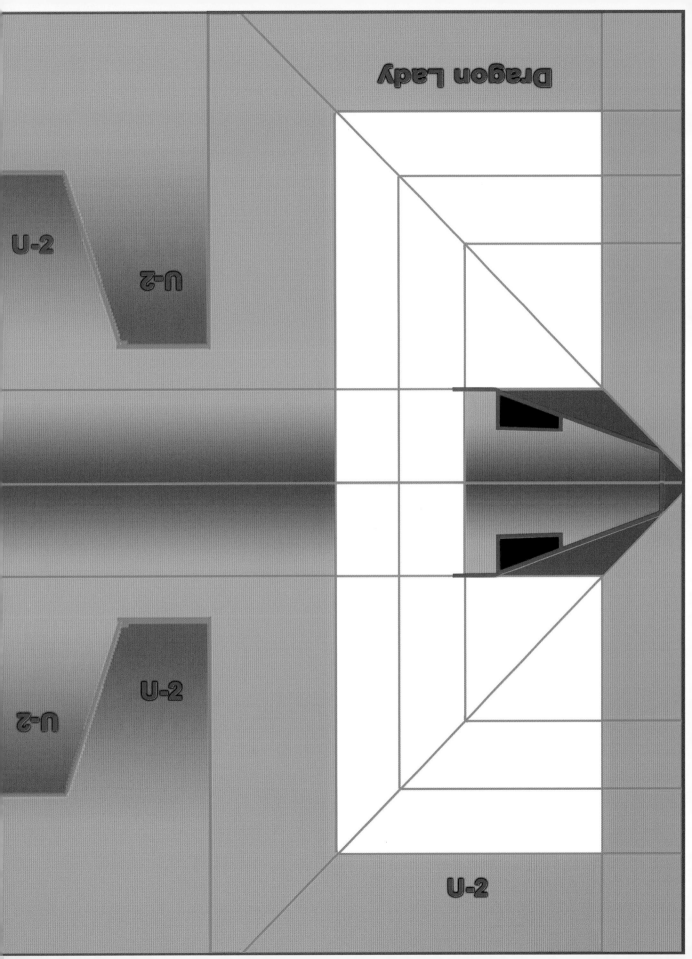

F-14 Tomcat

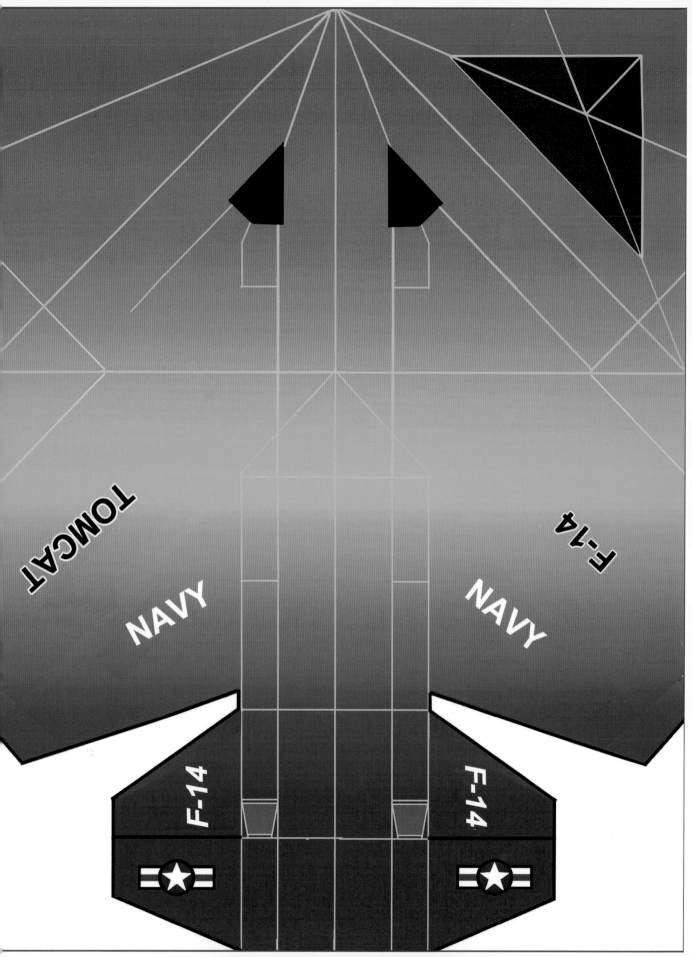

P-51 Mustang

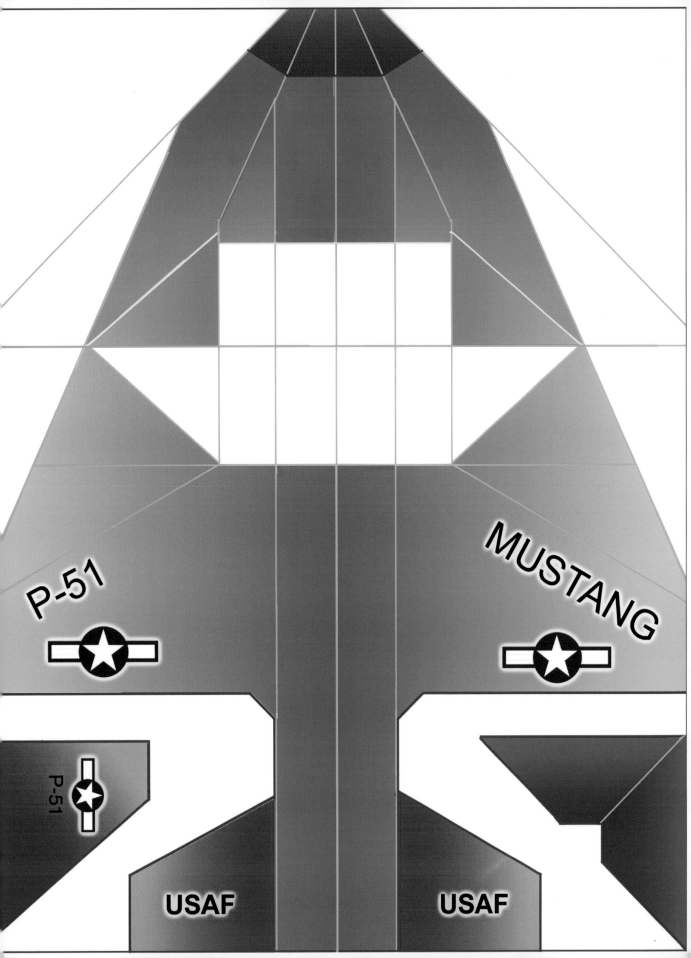

F-22 Raptor

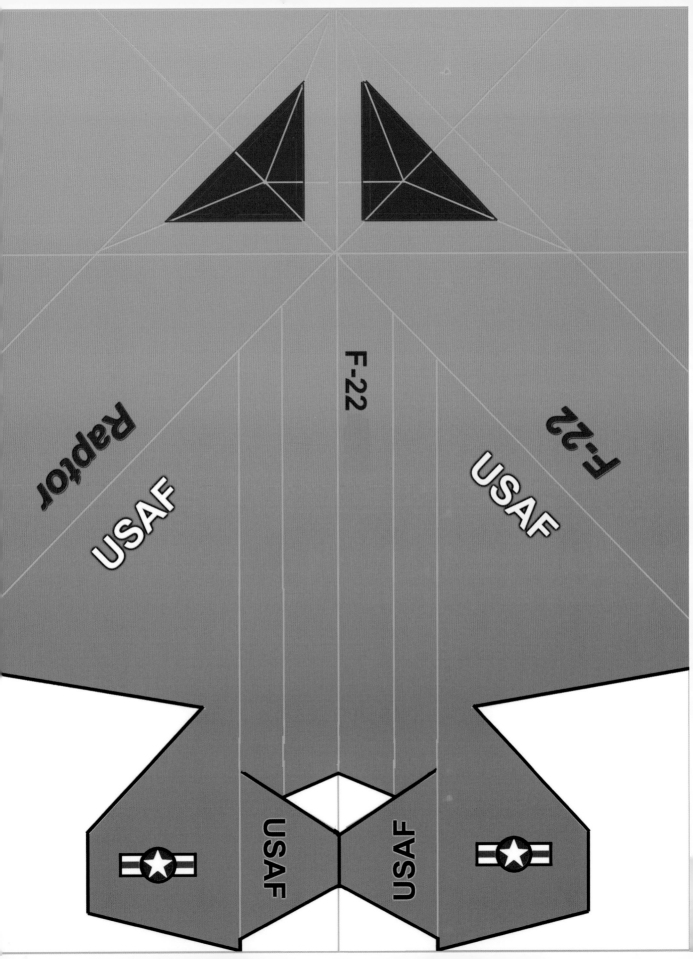

F-15 Eagle
Side A

Side A

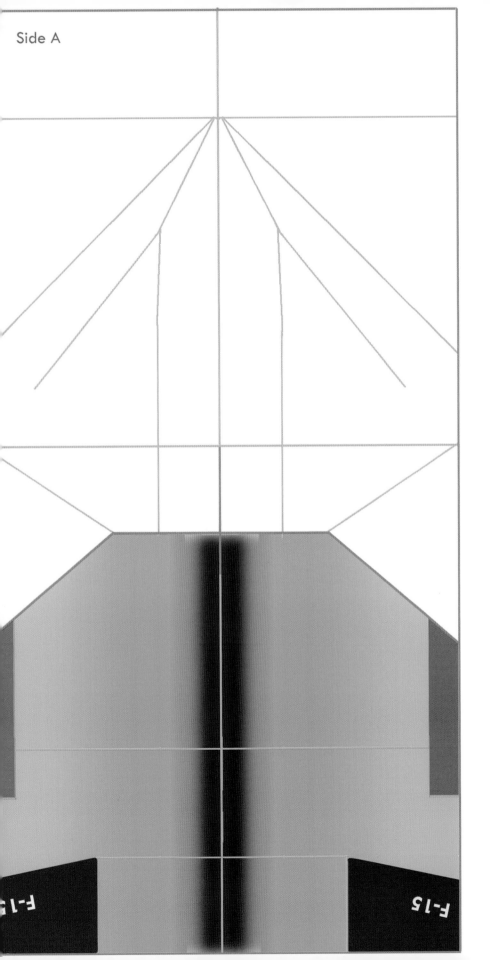

F-15   F-15

Side B

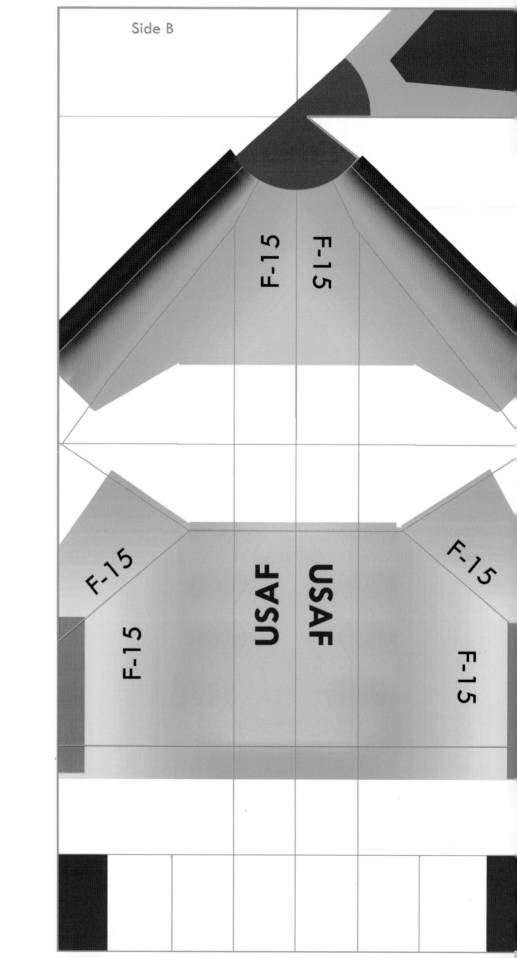

F-15 Eagle
Side B